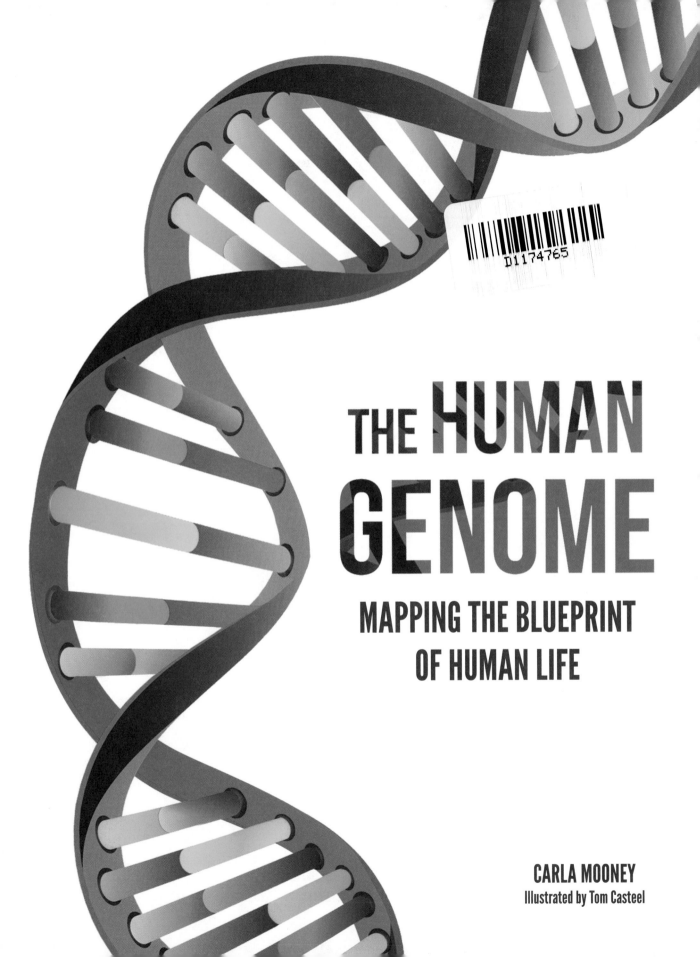

D1174765

THE HUMAN GENOME

MAPPING THE BLUEPRINT OF HUMAN LIFE

CARLA MOONEY
Illustrated by Tom Casteel

Nomad Press

A division of Nomad Communications

10 9 8 7 6 5 4 3 2 1

This book was manufactured by Versa Press, Inc., East Peoria, Illinois
June 2020, Job #J20-01719
ISBN Softcover: 978-1-61930-907-4
ISBN Hardcover: 978-1-61930-904-3

Educational Consultant, Marla Conn

Questions regarding the ordering of this book should be addressed to
Nomad Press
2456 Christian St., White River Junction, VT 05001
www.nomadpress.net

Printed in the United States.

Titles in the Inquire & Investigate
Human Beings set

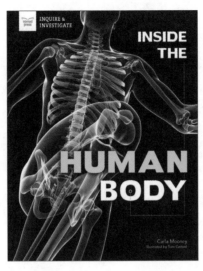

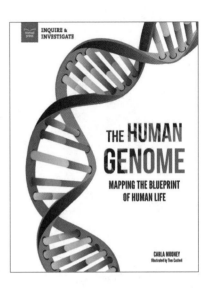

Check out more titles at www.nomadpress.net

Interested in primary sources?

PS

Look for this icon.

You can use a smartphone or tablet app to scan the QR codes and explore more! Cover up neighboring QR codes to make sure you're scanning the right one. You can find a list of URLs on the Resources page.

If the QR code doesn't work, try searching the internet with the Keyword Prompts to find other helpful sources.

🔍 human genome

Contents

Timeline VI

Introduction
The Code of Life 1

Chapter 1
How Genes Work 9

Chapter 2
The Race to Map the Human Genome 23

Chapter 3
What Does the Human Genome Tell Us? 41

Chapter 4
Using the Human Genome to Improve Health 57

Chapter 5
Human Evolution: The Story of Us 79

Chapter 6
Our Genomic Future 91

Glossary ▼ Metric Conversions ▼ Resources
Selected Bibliography ▼ Index

TIMELINE

1865: Gregor Mendel discovers "factors," or genes.

1869: Johann Friedrich Miescher extracts DNA from the nuclei of white blood cells.

1910: Thomas Hunt Morgan establishes the chromosomal theory of heredity.

1913: Alfred Sturtevant creates the first gene map.

1953: James Watson, Francis Crick, and Rosalind Franklin contribute to the discovery of the structure of DNA, a double helix.

1977: Fred Sanger and Walter Gilbert develop techniques to read and sequence chemical bases of DNA.

1983: Kary Mullis develops a copying machine to make copies of specific regions on DNA quickly in a test tube.

1983: The gene for Huntington's disease, a genetic disorder that affects muscle coordination and leads to cognitive and psychiatric problems, is located on chromosome 4.

1984: Alec Jeffreys develops DNA fingerprinting techniques that can be used to identify people and solve crimes.

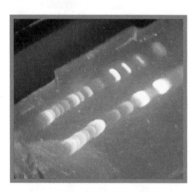

1984: The study of evolution at the DNA level begins.

1985: The gene for cystic fibrosis, a genetic disorder that often affects the lungs, is located on chromosome 7.

1986: Leroy Hood develops the automated sequencing machine.

1987: Scientists develop a genealogical tree that suggests all human mitochondrial DNA can be traced back to a common African maternal ancestor.

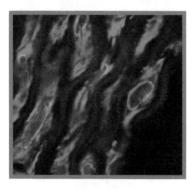

1988: The Human Genome Project begins with the goal of mapping the entire sequence of DNA in human chromosomes.

1990: Scientists propose to decode the human genome within 15 years.

1995: A small bacterium *H. influenzae* is sequenced.

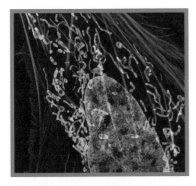

1996: A yeast genome is sequenced.

1998: The roundworm *C. elegans* is sequenced.

2000: U.S. President Bill Clinton announces that scientists have completed a first draft of the human genome.

2001: The first draft of the human genome sequence is published.

2002: The mouse genome is sequenced.

2002: The International HapMap Project launches to map common human genome variations by population group.

2003: The full sequence of the human genome is completed and published.

2003: The National Human Genome Research Institute launches a project named ENCODE to identify and describe all of the functional parts of the human genome.

2004: The rat genome is sequenced.

2005: The National Geographic Society and IBM launch a massive project to use DNA to map human migration during the last 60,000 years.

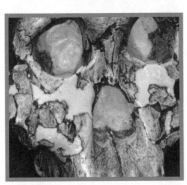

2008: The 1000 Genomes Project launches with the goal of sequencing more than 2,500 individuals from 26 different populations worldwide.

2008: DNA from a previously unknown line of ancient humans is extracted from a fossilized fingertip found in Denisova Cave in Russia.

2012: The ENCODE project publishes its results in a catalog of genetic data.

2017: Scientists are able to use CRISPR genome editing technology to correct a dangerous mutation in a human embryo and create a healthy embryo.

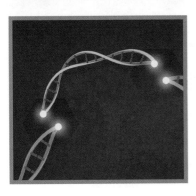

2019: Scientists adapt CRISPR genome editing technology to allow them to cut and splice large genome fragments more easily.

Introduction ▷

The Code of Life

What makes you different?

Our genes, passed down to offspring through biological parents, influence what we look like and even how we behave.

Have you ever wondered what makes you one of a kind? Why do you look and act a certain way? You might have your mom's blue eyes and your dad's brown hair. Maybe you don't resemble either parent but are the spitting image of your grandfather when he was your age.

How does your body know what color your hair and eyes should be, how tall you should grow, and countless other details that make you unique? For that matter, how does your body know that you should have two arms, two legs, and ten fingers and toes?

The answer lies in your human genome, the code of life.

A genome is the complete genetic code of an organism. An organism's genetic code is a set of instructions that holds all of the information necessary to develop, grow, and stay alive.

FOLLOW THE STEPS

Have you ever assembled a toy from a Lego kit? You open the bag, dump out the pieces, and follow the step-by-step instructions to put the Lego bricks together to build the toy. Just as the booklet of instructions shows you what to do, an organism's genome holds the instructions needed to build and sustain an organism.

Every living thing—every dog, tree, spider, and human—has its own unique genome. Every genome is different. No other organism alive has the same set of unique genetic instructions that you do.

However, even though each genome is unique, genomes are remarkably similar. In fact, every human genome is 99.9 percent the same. It's that tiny 0.1 percent that makes you different from your best friend, your brother, and your neighbor! Even organisms from different species share much of the same genome.

The human genome shares about 96 percent of its genome with that of chimpanzees.

For example, the human genome shares about 96 percent of its genome with chimpanzees. And more than 60 percent of the human genome is the same as a banana's genome. This sounds impossible—how can humans and bananas share the majority of their genome when they are so different? Actually, the instructions for making and sustaining life are very similar, whether they're for a human, fruit fly, dog—or banana.

Every genome is made of the same basic material, a macromolecule called deoxyribonucleic acid (DNA). DNA carries an organism's genetic information and is organized into segments called genes. A gene holds the instructions for a specific trait, such as hair or eye color.

One way to think of it is this: DNA is like the letters that make up words. Together, DNA's words form sentences, which are genes. Put it all together and it becomes a complete book, an entire genome.

The genes and DNA that make up a genome are passed down from an organism to its offspring. Your biological parents passed down their genetic information to you. For each trait, you inherited at least two copies of a gene—one from your mom and one from your dad. If you have your mom's eyes or your dad's hair, your genome explains why.

WHAT INFORMATION DOES THE HUMAN GENOME HOLD?

The human genome is made up of an estimated 20,000 to 25,000 genes! Genes hold instructions for making proteins that the body needs to grow and function. These proteins are responsible for traits such as eye color and hair color. They do most of the work in cells and are essential for the structure, function, and regulation of the body's organs and tissues.

Every time cells need to build a protein, they use the instructions coded into genes. For example, genes tell cells how to build a protein called actin, which is one of the building blocks of the body's muscles.

Although genes are essential to life, they are only a tiny part of the human genome, just 1 to 2 percent. A large part of the genome is noncoding, which means it is a sequence of DNA that does not code for a protein.

For a long time, scientists believed that noncoding parts of the human genome were junk DNA and had no function. Today, researchers know that many noncoding parts of the human genome have their own important jobs. For example, some of these areas are responsible for switching genes on and off. When a switch is turned on, it sends out instructions to make a protein. When the switch is turned off, the protein is not made.

AN IMPORTANT MYSTERY

The human genome has long been a mystery. While scientists knew it consisted of all an organism's genes and the DNA that made them, they did not know how to read its code. In recent years, scientists have made several breakthroughs in unlocking the mystery of the human genome. This knowledge has improved our understanding of how humans have evolved, how we are connected to other species, and the role of genes in disease.

The human genome printed out in book form

credit: Frankie Roberto (CC BY 2.0)

Watch a video about the mapping of the human genome. What does the race between the two competitors show about different scientific communities?

 TED-Ed Nguyen genome

VOCAB LAB

Write down what you think each word means. What root words can you find to help you? What does the context of the word tell you?

genes, **genome**, **noncoding**, **organism**, **protein**, and **trait**.

Compare your definitions with those of your friends or classmates. Did you all come up with the same meanings? Turn to the text and glossary if you need help.

In *The Human Genome*, we'll take a look at the fascinating world of genetics and the human genome. We'll learn the basics of how genes work, how DNA is structured, and how genetic inheritance works.

We'll explore the discoveries scientists have made about the human genome and how these discoveries have helped us better understand and treat certain diseases, trace our human ancestry and migration, and compare our species to others. In addition, we'll explore some of the ethical, legal, and social issues that arise from advances in genomic science. Together, we'll explore the mystery that is the human genome!

KEY QUESTIONS

- Why might scientists make mapping the human genome a priority?
- Why is the human genome so similar to the genomes of chimpanzees and even bananas?

EXTRACT DNA FROM A STRAWBERRY

Cells are the basic unit of life. Inside most cells, you'll find DNA. This large molecule carries all the genetic information for a cell. Simply put, DNA holds the instruction manual for life. Each DNA molecule looks like a long, thin thread. See for yourself!

- **To start, clean your strawberries and make sure there are no green leaves on them.** Put the strawberries into a plastic bag and seal it. Gently smash the berries for about 2 minutes until they are crushed.

- **In a plastic cup, mix together ½ cup of water, 2 teaspoons of dish detergent, and 1 teaspoon of salt.** Put 2 teaspoons of this extraction liquid in the plastic bag with the strawberries. Reseal the bag and gently crush the berries again for about a minute.

- **Place a coffee filter inside a clean plastic cup and pour the strawberry mixture into the filter.** Gently squeeze any liquid in the filter into the cup.

- **Estimate the amount of strawberry liquid in the cup.** Pour an equal amount of cold rubbing alcohol gently down the side of the cup (not directly into the cup). Do not mix or stir the mixture.

- **Examine the contents of the cup.** Use the coffee stirrer to help. What do you see? What does it look like? That is DNA!

Ideas for Supplies ▼

- strawberries
- plastic resealable sandwich bag
- 2 plastic cups
- dish detergent
- salt
- coffee filter
- rubbing alcohol
- coffee stirrer

To investigate more, try using a different berry or type of fruit in this experiment. What happens? Can you think of any other sources of DNA to experiment with?

Chapter 1 ▷
How Genes Work

Why is DNA so important?

DNA is the foundation of our genetic makeup, which makes us look the way we look and act the way we act! But it can also be affected by things outside the body, such as the environment.

To learn how genes work, we need to dive deep inside a human cell! And we have plenty of choices. The human body contains about 37 trillion cells. Inside nearly every cell, a copy of the human genome exists. Most of the DNA that makes up the human genome stays protected inside the cell's nucleus, while a tiny amount can be found in the cell's energy factories, called the mitochondria.

To better understand the human genome, we first need to understand the cell, DNA, and genes, and how they all work together.

Every living thing is made of cells. Cells are small units that hold all of the biological equipment and information needed for an organism to grow and stay alive.

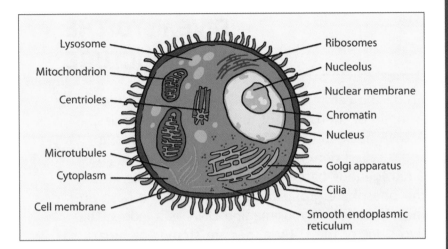

Lysosome
Mitochondrion
Centrioles
Microtubules
Cytoplasm
Cell membrane
Ribosomes
Nucleolus
Nuclear membrane
Chromatin
Nucleus
Golgi apparatus
Cilia
Smooth endoplasmic reticulum

Within a single organism, there may be many types of cells. In humans, there are hundreds of types of cells. Some cells form muscle or organ tissue, while other cells carry nutrients throughout the body. Understanding how cells work is an important part of learning about the human genome.

An animal cell, such as the ones you have in your body, look a little like a plastic bag that has a few tiny holes in it. This bag-like barrier is the cell membrane, and it holds all of the cell structures and fluid inside the cell and blocks unwanted materials from entering the cell. Tiny holes in the membrane allow some substances—such as nutrients and waste products—to move in and out of the cell.

Inside the cell membrane, several organelles float within a jelly-like fluid called cytoplasm. These organelles perform important functions, such as generating energy or building proteins.

A spherical object called the nucleus serves as the cell's command center. A nuclear membrane protects the nucleus and separates its contents from the rest of the cell. Most of the cell's genetic material, DNA, is found in the cell nucleus. It's a very important, tiny space!

GREGOR MENDEL: DISCOVERING HUMAN GENES

For centuries, scientists struggled to understand how traits were passed from parent to offspring. In the 1800s, an Austrian monk named Gregor Mendel (1822–1884) bred pea plants and performed experiments to study this mystery. After thousands of observations and many, many plants, Mendel concluded that heredity was controlled by factors that acted in pairs. Today, we know these factors as genes. Offspring receive one gene from each parent to make a pair. Mendel concluded that the factors that control traits could be dominant or recessive. A dominant trait masked the presence of a recessive trait. He also concluded that the factors that controlled traits were made of two distinct types of alleles. Today, Mendel is known as the "father of genetics." His work became the basis for the study of genes and genetics.

DIVE INTO THE DNA STRUCTURE

Inside the cell nucleus, the DNA macromolecule is made of thousands of units called nucleotides. A DNA nucleotide contains three components: a sugar called deoxyribose, a phosphate group, and a nitrogenous base. The sugar in the middle links the phosphate group on one side and the base on the other side. If you imagine DNA as a ladder, the two sides of the DNA ladder are strands of sugar and phosphate, while the bases extend out and link together to form the ladder's rungs. The DNA ladder is twisted into the shape of a double helix.

In each strand, DNA uses only four bases: adenine (A), thymine (T), guanine (G), and cytosine (C). When the bases link to form the DNA ladder's rungs, adenine always pairs with thymine, while guanine always pairs with cytosine. A strand of DNA can be millions of base pairs long.

DNA carries the instructions for making a cell's proteins, which enable living organisms to function. But how does DNA tell the cell what to do? What language do they use? How do all of the biological parts understand each other?

The order of DNA's four bases creates DNA's code and forms the basis of its language. It's the sequence of the bases and the length of the DNA strands that make each person and organism unique. No two humans, except for identical twins, have exactly the same sequence of bases in their DNA.

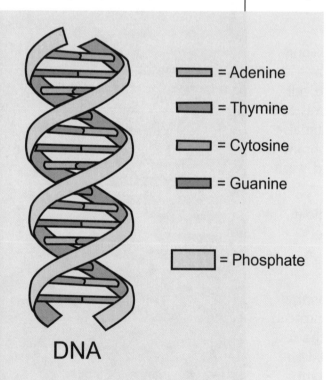

= Adenine

= Thymine

= Cytosine

= Guanine

= Phosphate

DNA

DNA REPLICATION— MAKING MORE

The human body makes new cells every day. Most cells with a nucleus (known as eukaryotic cells) follow a pattern of growth and division called the cell cycle. In the cell cycle, the cell grows in phases and divides in four phases to make new cells. This process of cell division is called mitosis. When the cell reproduces, it passes its DNA instructions to the newly created cells so they can follow the same function as the old cells.

Before a cell divides, it makes a copy of the DNA in its nucleus in a process called DNA replication. First, DNA's double helix structure splits apart down the middle to form two single strands of DNA. The bases on each strand act as a pattern to reform the other side of the ladder. Remember—adenine always pairs with thymine, while guanine always pairs with cytosine. New nucleotides move into each side of the unzipped ladder and pair with their complementary nucleotides on each strand. An enzyme seals the bases together and reforms DNA's double helix.

> One side of the ladder is from the old strand of DNA while the other side is newly created.

When DNA replication is complete, the cell contains two identical molecules of DNA. That's when the cell division process begins. The parent cell divides into two daughter cells and passes a copy of its DNA to each new cell. The process of mitosis ensures that every new cell has a perfect and complete set of DNA that is identical to the original parent cell.

MITOSIS

Prophase

Metaphase

Anaphase

Telophase

Cells go through four different phases during mitosis: prophase, metaphase, anaphase, and telophase.

GETTING TO KNOW CHROMOSOMES AND GENES

If all of the DNA in a single human cell was stretched out, it would be about 6½ feet long, about as long as a car. If long DNA strands floated aimlessly around the cell, they would become a hopelessly tangled mess! Instead, DNA is carefully packaged to fit inside the cell nucleus.

To fit inside the cell nucleus, long DNA strands wind around proteins called histones, like thread wraps around a spool. Each of these wrapped bundles is called a nucleosome. A chain of nucleosomes forms a chromatin. Under a powerful microscope, a chromatin can look like a long string of beads. A cell's chromatin loops and coils to form tightly condensed chromosomes. The tight packaging ensures DNA's long strands can fit neatly inside the cell nucleus.

In most human cells, there are 46 chromosomes, which come in 23 pairs. Each person inherits one complete set of chromosomes from their mom and another from their dad. The first 22 pairs of chromosomes are called autosomal chromosomes and are the same in males and females. The 23rd pair of chromosomes are the sex chromosomes, which determine the gender of a baby.

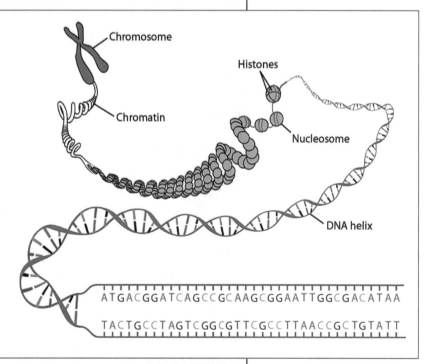

Chromosome

Histones

Chromatin

Nucleosome

DNA helix

ATGACGGATCAGCCGCAAGCGGAATTGGCGACATAA
TACTGCCTAGTCGGCGTTCGCCTTAACCGCTGTATT

credit: OpenStax (CC BY 4.0)

The end of each chromosome is capped by a telomere, which is made of densely packed, repetitive DNA. The telomere protects the chromosome's DNA instructions.

Using high-powered microscopes, scientists can study and compare the subtle differences between each chromosome. Chromosomes come in different sizes and each has a unique striping or banding pattern. The bands divide a chromosome into regions that scientists use to identify different sections of a chromosome. The location of a centromere, an indented region on a chromosome that helps to keep it aligned during cell division, also varies on different chromosomes. It can be in the middle or closer to the top or bottom of the chromosome.

> Scientists use these differences in size, banding pattern, and centromere position to identify a chromosome.

As part of their research, scientists sort chromosomes into matching pairs using a picture called a karyotype. With a microscope, they take a picture of a person's 46 chromosomes. Then, they rearrange the chromosomes by size and pair, each with its matching chromosome. When the karyotype is complete, a geneticist can study it for any genetic abnormalities.

There are sections of DNA on each chromosome called genes. Genes have chemical switches that turn on and off to make different kinds of proteins. Cell proteins determine the color of your eyes, the shape of your nose, and the size of your feet. On a single chromosome, there can be hundreds or thousands of genes.

MIESCHER'S NUCLEIN

Although Gregor Mendel's work showed that factors, or genes, from parents were what controlled traits in offspring, scientists did not know what an organism's genetic material was. In 1869, a Swiss medical student named Johann Friedrich Miescher (1844–1895) found DNA for the first time. He was working with white blood cells, in the form of pus from infected wounds, when he found a substance that he named nuclein. At the time, Miescher did not realize that his nuclein was actually the genetic material of an organism.

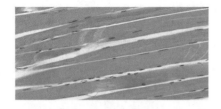

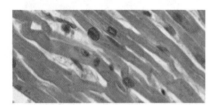

Muscle cells

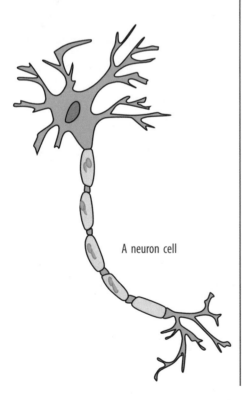

A neuron cell

In humans, each pair of chromosomes has two copies of the same gene. One copy of the gene came from the chromosome you inherited from your mother. The other copy came from the chromosome from your father. While the two genes are similar, they do not have to be identical. For example, both genes may control eye color. One form of the gene may lead to blue eyes, while the other form leads to brown eyes. Different versions of a gene are called alleles. Any gene can have one or more alleles.

Every time a cell needs to build a protein, they use the instructions coded by DNA into genes. For example, antibodies are proteins made by the body's immune system that bind to foreign bits of material, such as viruses and bacteria. Antibodies fight infections and protect the body from disease. If there is a problem with the gene that holds the instructions to build antibodies, the body may not be able to make antibodies properly. In some cases, this can lead to autoimmune diseases.

GENE REGULATION— WHAT TO DO, WHEN

Nearly every cell in the human body has a complete copy of your genome. Each cell holds the entire instruction manual for every process needed to sustain the body. Yet each cell in your body has a specific job. It only needs to read a small part of the DNA instruction manual to do its job. Think of a school with different teachers for math, literature, and science. Those teachers don't all have to know how to solve equations, how to diagram a sentence, and how to dissect a frog!

So, how does a cell decide which part of the manual to read and which genes to turn on?

Gene regulation determines which genes a cell uses and when to activate them.

For example, a muscle cell turns on the genes that make muscle fibers. Nerve cells would not turn on those genes because making muscles is not part of their job. Genes turn on when they are needed and turn off when they are not. Often, genes turn on as a response to a stimulus. Some genes turn on in response to cues from the cells around them. Others turn on because of stimuli in the external environment—for example, heat and light can act as stimuli. Other genes turn on at certain points in human development and turn off at other points.

GENETIC TRAITS

When the subject of genetics comes up, there's a lot of talk about traits. A trait is a feature or quality in a person. There are physical traits, such as the color of a person's hair, their height, or the size of their nose. A trait can also be behavioral. Some traits influence whether a person has an increased risk of getting a disease, including cancer, heart disease, and diabetes. Every human has different combinations of traits that have been passed down from their ancestors.

Genes carry instructions for traits. Some traits are controlled by a single pair of genes. For example, the color of your eyes is a trait controlled by a single pair of genes. Some people have blue eyes, while others have brown or green eyes.

There are two alleles for the gene that controls eye color. F represents the allele for brown eyes, while f represents the allele for blue. A person who has two ff alleles will have blue eyes. A person with two FF alleles will have brown eyes.

	F	f
F	FF	Ff
f	Ff	ff

A Punnett square is used to see how traits are expressed.

What about a person who has one of each allele (Ff)? When this occurs, one allele is usually dominant over a recessive allele. The dominant allele masks the recessive allele. In this case, the allele for brown eyes (F) is dominant, masking the recessive allele for blue eyes (f). The person with (Ff) alleles will have brown eyes.

Most traits are not this simple and are controlled by several genes. The genes may be located at different places on the same chromosome or even on different chromosomes.

Sometimes, the environment can affect traits. For example, genes determine hair color. But do you know anyone who dyes their hair? Sometimes, hair changes color when the person spends a lot of time in the sun, too. Even if a person's genes determine a person has blond hair, their hair might not always be blond.

Another example of environmental influence has to do with health. Do you eat plenty of vegetables and get enough exercise? Healthy habits can reduce the risk of disease. A person with a trait that makes them more likely to develop heart disease can lessen this risk by eating healthfully and exercising.

Eating healthfully is a major part of staying healthy!

THE GENETIC CODE

In the human body, there are trillions of cells, each of which is responsible for a specific job. Within each cell, there are thousands of proteins working together to run the cell like a well-oiled machine. In muscle cells, special proteins called actin and myosin allow the cells to contract. Proteins in the stomach called enzymes digest food. Growth hormones are proteins that tell the bones to grow. Proteins also carry out bodily functions such as respiration and digestion. DNA's genetic code tells the cell how to build all of these proteins. Cells are very busy places!

So, how does DNA send its message to make a protein? While proteins come in many shapes and sizes, every single one is a chain of amino acids. Amino acids are organic compounds that contain nitrogen and carbon. In the human body, there are 20 amino acids that link together in thousands of combinations to create proteins. These amino acid chains fold into complex shapes and hook together. The order of amino acids in the chain determines the shape, properties, and function of a protein.

> A single protein molecule can have as many as 5,000 amino acids.

DNA's sequence of nucleotide bases is the code that tells the cell what amino acids are needed and what order to place them in to make each protein in a process called translation. The DNA bases are read in groups of three, called codons. There are 64 possible three-base combinations, which is more than enough to code for 20 amino acids. Sometimes, multiple codons code for the same protein. Other codons signal where to start making the protein and where to stop.

FINDING DNA

By the mid-1900s, many scientists believed that a macromolecule called DNA held an organism's genetic information. But they still did not know what DNA looked like or how it worked. In 1949, Austrian scientist Erwin Chargaff (1905–2002) studied DNA in several organisms and discovered something they all had in common: Every DNA molecule had four nitrogen bases—adenine, cytosine, guanine, and thymine.

In the early 1950s, British scientists Rosalind Franklin (1920–1958) and Maurice Wilkins (1916–2004) bounced X-rays off a DNA molecule to see what it looked like. The process created a shadow picture that showed the DNA molecule looked like a ladder with rungs that twisted in a spiral helix shape. At the same time, American scientist James Watson (1928–) and British scientist Francis Crick (1916–2004) were building models to help them understand DNA's structure. Combining Franklin's findings and Chargaff's research, Watson and Crick realized that the DNA molecule was made of two chains of nucleotides that were paired to form a double helix. For their work, Watson, Crick, and Wilkins received the Nobel Prize in Medicine in 1962.

TYPES OF RNA

There are three types of RNA in the cell.

Messenger RNA (mRNA) carries information from the DNA in the cell nucleus to the ribosomes in the cytoplasm.

Ribosomal RNA (rRNA) is the structural part of ribosomes

Transfer RNA (tRNA) carries amino acids to the ribosome to help build an amino acid chain.

The first step in decoding a genetic message to make a protein is transcription. During transcription, a molecule inside the cell unzips the DNA and copies one strand of the unzipped DNA into messenger RNA (mRNA). Like DNA, RNA is a nucleotide made up of a sugar, a phosphate group, and a nitrogenous base. Unlike DNA, RNA uses the sugar ribose and is generally a single strand. In RNA, the base thymine is replaced by uracil.

These differences help enzymes in the cell tell the difference between DNA and RNA.

The original DNA strands reconnect, and mRNA carries DNA's message out of the nucleus to ribosomes in the cell's cytoplasm. The ribosomes read the message carried by mRNA and translate each codon into one of 20 possible amino acids.

Another type of RNA, called transfer RNA (tRNA), carries the specific amino acid to the ribosome, where it is linked into a chain with other amino acids. When complete, the chain of amino acids folds into a specific three-dimensional structure. The completed protein is now ready for its job in the human body.

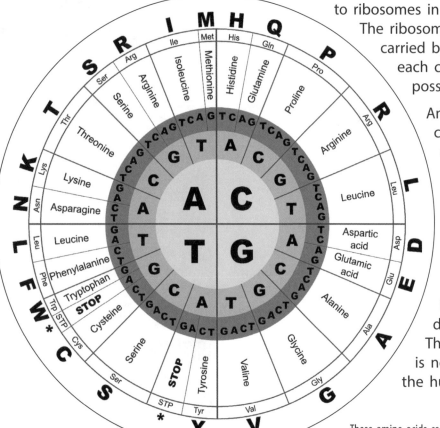

These amino acids correspond to the nucleotide bases.

These twins have identical DNA!

As you can see, genetics is a complicated subject with lots of parts and processes. To help keep track of genes, scientists have come up with a way of mapping them, so they can know what gene corresponds to which trait. In the next chapter, we'll take a look at the map of the human genome.

KEY QUESTIONS

- If our traits—both behavioral and physical—are influenced by our genes, what responsibilities do humans have to control what we do and say?

- What can you do to support the healthy genes in your body?

VOCAB LAB

Write down what you think each word means. What root words can you find to help you? What does the context of the word tell you?

allele, chromosome, dominant, mitosis, nucleotide, organelles, recessive, transcription, and **translation.**

Compare your definitions with those of your friends or classmates. Did you all come up with the same meanings? Turn to the text and glossary if you need help.

TEXT TO WORLD

What are some of the environmental factors in your life that can contribute to your own cell health?

genetic code

UniProt

DECODING DNA'S MESSAGE

Try transcribing and translating a DNA sequence into an amino acid chain and then find the matching protein. You'll need to access the Universal Genetic Code and the UniProt database of proteins from the internet to do this project.

- **When transcription begins, a portion of the DNA ladder unzips so that mRNA can copy the gene's sequence of nucleotide bases.** Start with this sequence of unzipped DNA:

  GGTTGGGCTTTGCGGATCATGTTTCTACATCTGTAC

- **Now, transcribe the DNA into mRNA.** Determine the sequence of bases in the complementary strand of mRNA that would form next to this DNA strand. Remember that mRNA uses the base uracil (U) instead of thymine (T).

- **Using the Universal Genetic Code,** translate the mRNA message into a chain of amino acids.

- **What protein does this amino acid chain create?** Enter the DNA nucleotide sequence (not the transcribed mRNA sequence) into the BLAST tool in the UniProt database of proteins to find out. You could also enter the amino acid sequence into the tool. A BLAST search allows scientists to compare an amino acid sequence to database records. This helps them find the closest matching protein to help them figure out what protein it is and how it functions. Filter your results by "Reviewed" entries only.

- **What is the name of the protein?** What gene encodes for it? What organism uses this protein? What is its function? Why is this protein relevant to humans?

To investigate more, explore how you could change the DNA genetic code without affecting the resulting protein. In what circumstances could changes to the DNA genetic code occur?

Chapter 2 ▷
The Race to Map the Human Genome

Why is it useful to have a map of the human genome?

Once we know what genes affect which areas of life and health, scientists can better treat diseases and offer instructions on how individuals can stay healthy.

Understanding how DNA and genes carry the code for life is just the beginning. There is so much more to learn and understand about the human genome! How many genes do humans have? Which genes control specific traits? And how are genes linked to disease?

The answers to these questions and more lie inside the human genome. But trying to understand the human genome is like trying to read a book written in a secret code! In order to reveal the book's secrets, you first have to find the coded message.

When dealing with the human genome, the coded message is the order of DNA's nucleotide bases—all of the As, Cs, Gs, and Ts. If nucleotides are like the letters in a message, learning the order of the bases can get scientists one step closer to reading DNA's words. Let's take a closer look.

GENOME SEQUENCING

The process of determining the order of DNA's nucleotide bases is called DNA sequencing. Genome sequencing is figuring out the order of the DNA bases in an entire genome. In the human genome, that's more than 3 billion bases. It's so big that scientists have to break it into smaller pieces to tackle the task.

They sequence the smaller pieces and then put them back together in the right order to determine the sequence of the entire genome. It's like putting together a gigantic genetic jigsaw puzzle.

There are two approaches to cutting up the genome and putting it back together again. One approach is called "clone-by-clone" sequencing. During this approach, scientists create a map of each chromosome in the genome. Then, they break the DNA into large chunks called clones, which are about 150,000 base pairs long. The location of each clone on the chromosome is mapped to help assemble them in order after sequencing.

Scientists cut each clone into smaller, overlapping pieces that are about 500 base pairs long. They sequence these pieces and use the overlaps to reconstruct the sequence of the entire clone, in order. Computers carry out the reconstruction by identifying the overlapping areas and piecing the DNA sequence back together.

NANOPORE DNA SEQUENCING

Scientists are constantly looking for ways to improve DNA and genome sequencing. One technology in development uses nanopores to sequence DNA. Nanopore DNA sequencing takes a single DNA strand and threads it through an extremely tiny pore in a membrane. As the strand squeezes through the nanopore, the DNA bases are read one by one. The bases are identified by measuring their effect on an electrical current flowing through the pore. Nanopore DNA sequencing offers several advantages over current methods. For example, nanopore DNA sequencing can process very long DNA segments and produce long reads. The longer a segment reads, the greater chance it will overlap with another segment. This makes assembling the genome in the correct order much easier. Like a puzzle, when the puzzle pieces are larger, it is easier to put them together. Additionally, nanopore DNA sequencing allows scientists to study the same molecule repeatedly, unlike other DNA sequencing methods.

By following the map created at the beginning, the computers put the large chunks back together as part of the complete genome sequence.

Another genome sequencing approach is called the "whole-genome shotgun" method. In shotgun sequencing, the whole genome is broken up into small pieces of DNA for sequencing. The DNA fragments vary in size from 2,000 to 300,000 base pairs. Once sequenced, the DNA fragments are reassembled by a computer that looks for areas where the fragments overlap.

Shotgun sequencing is like shredding multiple copies of a book, mixing up all of the pieces, and putting the book back together by finding pieces with text that overlap.

Each approach to genome sequencing has advantages and disadvantages. While the clone-by-clone method is very reliable, it is also slow and expensive. The mapping stage in particular can be very time consuming.

In comparison, the whole-genome shotgun method is much faster, but it can be extremely difficult to put all of the DNA pieces back together. Plus, the whole-genome shotgun method only works when there is a reference genome—a previously sequenced genome example—that scientists can use as a guide when they are reassembling the vast number of DNA pieces.

HOW DNA SEQUENCING WORKS

Let's take a look at how one kind of DNA sequencing works. The Sanger sequencing method uses a technique called gel electrophoresis to separate pieces of DNA that differ in length by just one base.

In gel electrophoresis, scientists place DNA fragments at one end of a gel. There are electrodes at each end of the gel. When scientists apply an electrical current to the gel, one end of the gel has a positive charge, while the other has a negative charge. This causes the negatively charged DNA molecules to move through the gel toward the positive end. Smaller fragments move through the gel faster, which causes the DNA fragments to separate according to size.

Until the late 1980s, electrophoresis gels were read by a person. Each piece of DNA was attached to a radioactive label that appeared as a band. An X-ray picture was made of the gel to show the positions of the DNA bands. Scientists carefully analyzed the rows and columns of DNA bands on the gel so they could determine the sequence of the DNA. The process was very slow and tedious!

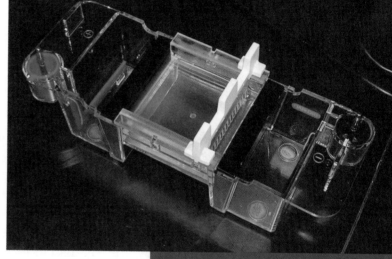

Gel box for electrophoresis with gel inside
credit: Joseph Elsbernd (CC BY 2.0)

Today, automatic sequencing machines have made large-scale sequencing projects possible. These machines became available in the late 1980s and have made DNA sequencing much faster and more accurate. Most automatic sequencing machines work like the manual sequencing process. As the DNA pieces move through the gel, the machine reads the order of the bases and stores this information in its computer. The sequence data that comes out of an automated sequencing machine is raw. The short DNA sequences are jumbled together like the pieces of a jigsaw puzzle. They still have to be put together to make a picture of the genome.

Assembling the pieces of sequenced DNA into a complete genome is done by computer programs known as assemblers. These programs assemble DNA sequences by finding and analyzing areas of the DNA sequence that overlap. The end result is a large section of the genome that is assembled correctly. The process is like putting a jigsaw puzzle together. The assembler places the DNA puzzle pieces next to each other to see if they fit—if they do, it snaps the pieces together.

IS THIS RIGHT?

How do scientists know a genome sequence is correct? When a genome has never been sequenced before, it's a little bit like exploring new territory. There is nothing to compare the results with to double check if the sequence is correct. To make it even trickier, errors can pop up at any point during the sequencing process—when the DNA is cut into fragments, when it is copied, as it goes through the sequencing machine, or as it is assembled back together. Plenty of chances to make mistakes!

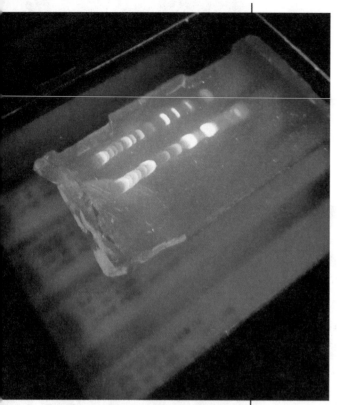

Two different DNA ladders appearing in the gel

credit: Joseph Elsbernd (CC BY 2.0)

To minimize the chance of errors, scientists repeat the sequencing process multiple times.

They sequence multiple copies of a genome so that each base is sequenced many times. That way, even if there is an error during one of the sequencing processes, it is likely that there will be other, correct reads that provide an accurate sequence.

Plus, automatic sequencing machine software looks for bases that seem out of place, spots that could be an error. Low-quality reads that have a lot of errors are removed before assembly. Sometimes, this is done manually by scientists—other times it is handled automatically by the computer.

Another way scientists avoid mistakes is by having the assembler software compare the multiple reads of the same part of DNA to create a "consensus" sequence. For example, if a certain base is read as a T nine times and is read as a G on the 10th time, the G reading is probably a mistake. The assembler evaluates the different reads and decides which is likely to be correct.

Once a sequence is assembled, it can be checked against small parts of the genome that have been previously sequenced and assembled. If the assembly matches with other known sequences, it's probably accurate.

BUILDING UP THE HUMAN GENOME

The human genome is enormous, about 3 billion base pairs. Before scientists could tackle the immense task of sequencing the human genome, they first gained experience working with smaller genomes. Organisms with smaller genomes allowed scientists to develop and test sequencing technologies, laboratory techniques, and tools that would be needed to sequence the human genome.

In 1995, a team of scientists led by Claire Fraser (1955–) and J. Craig Venter (1946–) from the Institute for Genomic Research in Maryland decided to sequence a small bacterium, *Haemophilus influenzae*.

To sequence your entire genome, scientists need less than a teaspoon of your blood or saliva.

GENE GENIUS

The sequencing of *Haemophilus influenzae's* genome led to a vaccine that has reduced the number of cases of bacterial meningitis and ear infections in children.

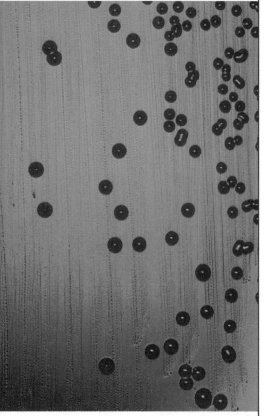

Haemophilus influenzae

H. influenzae was discovered in 1892 during an influenza epidemic. Although it does not cause influenza (as was originally thought), the bacterium does cause bacterial meningitis, middle-ear infections, and pneumonia. Like many bacteria, the genome of *H. influenzae* is held in a single, circular chromosome. To sequence the bacterium's genome, the scientists cut its DNA into fragments. Each fragment was about 1,000 to 2,000 base pairs long. Using high-powered computers and software programs, the scientists sequenced *H. influenzae*'s 1.8 million base pairs. It was the first complete sequencing of a free-living organism.

After the bacterium's genome was sequenced, the scientists searched for the genes that encoded its proteins and determined their functions. In bacteria, a single section of DNA that encodes a protein is almost always an entire gene. There are few sequences of noncoding DNA in bacteria.

Finding a gene in a bacterium is easier than finding a gene in a human.

Still, it was a painstaking process to identify the more than 1,700 genes in the *H. influenzae* genome. Scientists compared gene sequences in *H. influenzae* to genes whose functions were already known in other species. This allowed them to assign functions to more than 1,000 of the bacterium's genes. Some of the genes that could not be identified are the ones that make *H. influenzae* different from other species.

After the success with *H. influenzae*, scientists chose other small organisms to sequence. The sequencing process taught them valuable lessons and helped them master techniques that they would use to sequence larger genomes. In 1997, scientists were able to sequence *E. coli* and identify its 4,288 genes.

GOING AROUND THE ROUNDWORM

In 1998, *Caenorhabditis elegans* became the first multicellular organism to have its genome completely sequenced. *C. elegans* is a tiny roundworm that measures only 1 millimeter in length. Although it only has about 1,000 cells in its body, *C. elegans* has several different specialized organs—just like humans. It has nervous and digestive systems and a reproductive system.

Like humans, *C. elegans* starts life as a single fertilized cell. It develops as an embryo until it becomes a fully formed animal. Because the creature is transparent, it is easy for scientists to study and watch the worm's body systems as they work.

Scientists at the Sanger Institute in England and at Washington University in St. Louis, Missouri, discovered nearly 20,000 genes on the roundworm's six chromosomes. Sequencing *C. elegans* contributed much to genetic research. The worm's chromosomes are more like human chromosomes than those of bacteria. In fact, about 40 percent of the worm's genes are similar to genes in humans.

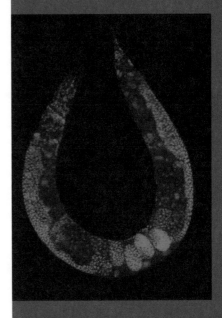

PCR TECHNOLOGY

Another advance that brought scientists one step closer to sequencing the entire human genome was the introduction of polymerase chain reaction (PCR) technology in 1983. Developed by American biochemist Kary Mullis (1944–2019), PCR is a technique that can be used to make many copies or to amplify a section of DNA. Using PCR, scientists can make millions of copies of a section of DNA from a very small amount of DNA. PCR is quick and cheap— sometimes, scientists call it molecular photocopying.

GENE GENIUS

Polymerase chain reaction (PCR) is heralded as one of the most important discoveries in molecular biology history. Its creator, Kary Mullis, won the Nobel Prize for Chemistry in 1993 for work with PCR. PCR is used in several lab and clinical techniques, including DNA fingerprinting, detection of bacteria or viruses, and diagnosis of genetic disorders.

Without PCR's ability to make many copies of a section of DNA, genetic studies that require large amounts of a DNA sample would be nearly impossible. Once copied, the DNA produced by PCR can be used in many different laboratory procedures.

Most mapping work in the Human Genome Project (HGP) used PCR.

PCR works by taking a sample of a DNA segment and heating it so the DNA separates into two pieces of single-strand DNA. Next, an enzyme called taq polymerase builds two new strands of DNA. It uses the original, separated DNA strands as a template. The process produces two exact copies of the original DNA strand, each containing one strand of old and one strand of new DNA. These two strands can then be used to create two more copies.

This cycle is called denaturing and synthesizing, or separating and building. Denaturing and synthesizing new DNA can repeat as many as 30 or 40 times and produce more than 1 billion exact copies of the original segment of DNA.

With today's lab technology, the cycling process is automated and can be finished in a few hours. A machine called a thermocycler is programmed to adjust the temperature of the reaction every few minutes, which causes the DNA to denature and synthesize.

TACKLING THE HUMAN GENOME

Since the discovery of DNA's structure in 1953, scientists have learned how the DNA code works to instruct the cell to build proteins. However, decoding pieces of human DNA was very difficult.

PCR AND THE PAST

Today, PCR technology is routinely being used for a wide variety of applications. One use for PCR is in archaeology. Scientists are using PCR technology to analyze and identify human and animal remains, including insects trapped in amber. PCR allows scientists to track human migration patterns and reconstruct degraded DNA samples. PCR even allows scientists to determine relationships between different species and differentiate between similar organisms.

To find a gene related to a disease, scientists examined a piece of DNA and manually decoded a few hundred bases—this took a whole day. According to Dr. Robert Waterston (1943–), a pioneer in DNA mapping, the process was very time consuming. They used to read the DNA bases on printouts after sequencing and then write them down on a piece of paper or manually enter them into a computer.

Scientists wanted a map of the entire human genome so they could locate genes that caused certain changes, such as those involved in deafness, Alzheimer's disease, cancer, and other illnesses. But at such a slow decoding rate, it would be nearly impossible. A breakthrough came when a machine was invented to computerize the entire process.

> Instead of decoding a few hundred bases by hand each day, the machines could decode a thousand bases every second. Phew!

With the ability to amplify sections of DNA to make sequencing easier and automated machines to make decoding DNA faster, the stage was finally set to tackle an immense project—sequencing the human genome. In 1984, the U.S. Department of Energy announced it would fund the sequencing of the entire human genome. They named the effort the Human Genome Project (HGP).

It was a huge project, but by 1987, the project's statement of purpose was clear. Scientists hoped that by understanding the human genome, they would be able to make further advances in medicine and other health sciences.

WHAT IS A GENOME MAP?

Genome mapping is used to find and mark the location of genes and the distance between genes on a chromosome. A genome map highlights the key landmarks in an organism's genome. Just like a map of New York City helps a tourist get around, a genome map helps scientists find their way around an organism's genome. The landmarks on a genome map include short DNA sequences, regulatory sites that turn genes one and off, and identified genes. A genome map is less detailed than a genome sequence that identifies the order of every DNA base. Often, a genome map is a work-in-progress. Scientists add information to the map as they make new discoveries. Genome maps help scientists assemble genome sequences. They also help scientists find new genes, particularly those involved in disease.

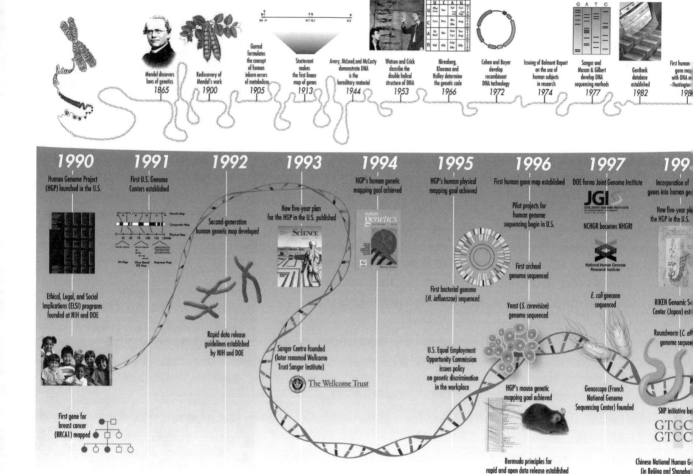

Mendel discovers laws of genetics
1865

Rediscovery of Mendel's work
1900

Garrod formulates the concept of human inborn errors of metabolism
1905

Sturtevant makes the first linear map of genes
1913

Avery, McLeod, and McCarty demonstrate DNA is the hereditary material
1944

Watson and Crick describe the double helical structure of DNA
1953

Nirenberg, Khorana and Holley determine the genetic code
1966

Cohen and Boyer develop recombinant DNA technology
1972

Issuing of Belmont Report on the use of human subjects in research
1974

Sanger and Maxam & Gilbert develop DNA sequencing methods
1977

GenBank database established
1982

First human gene map with DNA ma —Huntington
198...

1990
Human Genome Project (HGP) launched in the U.S.

Ethical, Legal, and Social Implications (ELSI) programs founded at NIH and DOE

First gene for breast cancer (BRCA1) mapped

1991
First U.S. Genome Centers established

Second-generation human genetic map developed

Rapid data release guidelines established by NIH and DOE

1992
New five-year plan for the HGP in the U.S. published

Sanger Centre founded (later renamed Wellcome Trust Sanger Institute)

The Wellcome Trust

1993
HGP's human genetic mapping goal achieved

SCIENCE

1994
HGP's human physical mapping goal achieved

nature genetics

First bacterial genome (H. influenzae) sequenced

U.S. Equal Employment Opportunity Commission issues policy on genetic discrimination in the workplace

1995
First human gene map established

Pilot projects for human genome sequencing begin in U.S.

First archael genome sequenced

Yeast (S. cerevisiae) genome sequenced

HGP's mouse genetic mapping goal achieved

Bermuda principles for rapid and open data release established

1996
DOE forms Joint Genome Institute

JGI
DOE JOINT GENOME INSTITUTE

NCHGR becomes NHGRI

National Human Genome Research Institute

E. coli genome sequenced

Genoscope (French National Genome Sequencing Center) founded

1997
Incorporation of genes into human ge...

New five-year pla... the HGP in the U.S...

RIKEN Genomic S... Center (Japan) est...

Roundworm (C. el... genome sequen...

SNP initiative be...

GTGC
GTCC

Chinese National Human G... (in Beijing and Shanghai...

199...

In 1990, the U.S. Department of Energy and the National Institutes of Health (NIH) teamed up to fund the project. James Watson, who was part of the team that discovered DNA's structure, was appointed the head of the NIH program. Watson encouraged the project to expand to include many other countries and enlisted the help of scientists around the world.

As high-powered computers and automated sequencing machines churned, the HGP's leaders felt confident that they would be able to complete sequencing the entire human genome in 15 years.

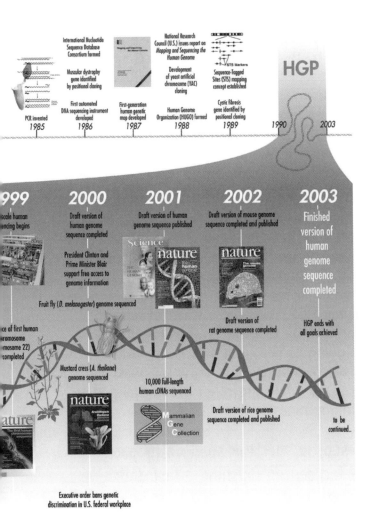

International Nucleotide Sequence Database Consortium formed

Muscular dystrophy gene identified by positional cloning

National Research Council (U.S.) issues report on Mapping and Sequencing the Human Genome

Development of yeast artificial chromosome (YAC) cloning

Sequence-Tagged Sites (STS) mapping concept established

HGP

First automated DNA sequencing instrument developed

First-generation human genetic map developed

Human Genome Organization (HUGO) formed

Cystic fibrosis gene identified by positional cloning

| PCR invented 1985 | 1986 | 1987 | 1988 | 1989 | 1990 | 2003 |

1999
scale human ncing begins

2000
Draft version of human genome sequence completed

President Clinton and Prime Minister Blair support free access to genome information

Fruit fly (D. melanogaster) genome sequenced

2001
Draft version of human genome sequence published

2002
Draft version of mouse genome sequence completed and published

2003
Finished version of human genome sequence completed

HGP ends with all goals achieved

ce of first human romosome mosome 22) completed

Mustard cress (A. thaliana) genome sequenced

Draft version of rat genome sequence completed

10,000 full-length human cDNAs sequenced

Mammalian Gene Collection

Draft version of rice genome sequence completed and published

to be continued..

Executive order bans genetic discrimination in U.S. federal workplace

As the work progressed, the scientists leading the project, along with representatives from the government and philanthropic agencies funding it, met to discuss the project's progress. In 1996, the group agreed that the human genome sequence was everyone's property.

All sequence information would be freely available in the public domain in order to support research and development and benefit society.

In 1998, an American company named Celera Genomics, led by the former Institute for Genomic Research scientist J. Craig Venter, entered the race to map the human genome. A Navy veteran, Venter had worked for the NIH, where he developed faster ways to read genes. He also started the Institute for Genomic Research, a not-for-profit organization that developed the shotgun approach for sequencing DNA.

Remember, the shotgun approach involved randomly dividing a genome, sequencing each part, and then putting it all back together. Scientists at Celera planned to use the whole-genome shotgun approach on the human genome. They believed this approach would allow them to finish sequencing faster than the HGP. However, instead of releasing the sequencing data to all as HGP planned to do, Celera was going to license it and file patents on interesting discoveries. Do you think this was the right thing to do when the other group planned to share the information for free?

In response, the HGP sped up its pace and focused on finishing a first draft, with details to be filled in later.

The HGP used DNA from a group of randomly chosen people from Buffalo, New York. The HGP scientists first mapped the genome and then sequenced it.

THE RACE IS ON!

The HGP and the Celera project were different in several ways. The HGP was funded by the government. A collaboration of scientists from universities and government agencies worked on it. Francis Collins (1950–), a professor of internal medicine and genetics at the University of Michigan, led research teams that found the gene mutations for several diseases, including cystic fibrosis, a hereditary disease that affects the lungs and digestive systems.

In 1993, Collins took over the National Human Genome Research Institutes and led the HGP. Collins and his team published their findings on the internet because they believed the information should be freely available to help other scientists develop medicines and treatments for a variety of diseases and disorders.

> Unlike the HGP, the Celera project was funded by a private company.

They used the information published by the HGP on the internet in their work, but did not publish their findings. Celera used DNA from five people of different races: two Caucasians, one Hispanic, one African American, and one person of Chinese background.

In June 2000, U.S. President Bill Clinton (1946–) held a press conference at the White House and announced that the two groups had simultaneously completed the first map of the entire human genome. "Without a doubt, this is the most important wondrous map ever produced by humankind," said Clinton. Before an audience of scientists, members of the U.S. Congress, health care advocates, and ambassadors from several countries, Clinton declared that the project's completion "is a stunning, humbling achievement."

In February 2001, the International Human Genome Sequencing Consortium published the first draft of the human genome. It included the sequence of the entire genome's 3 billion base pairs that was about 90 percent complete. The full sequence was completed and published in April 2003.

The sequenced human genome is not that of one person, but is a composite genome taken from several individuals.

Take a look at how the Sanger sequencing method works in this video.

 HHMI bio Sanger sequence

Write down what you think each word means. What root words can you find to help you? What does the context of the word tell you?

DNA sequencing, **fragment**, **gel electrophoresis**, **polymerase chain reaction**, **reference genome**, **sequence**, and **synthesize**.

Compare your definitions with those of your friends or classmates. Did you all come up with the same meanings? Turn to the text and glossary if you need help.

TEXT TO WORLD

Do you or anyone you know have a genetic disease? How does that affect everyday life?

The international effort to sequence the 3 billion base pairs in the human genome is considered by many to be one of the most significant scientific achievements of all time. Do you think it would have happened as quickly without the competition between the two groups working on the challenge?

The map of the human genome revealed some surprising information about human DNA. Scientists had thought humans had about 150,000 genes.

With the new map, they realized that a human has only about 20,000 to 25,000 genes.

They also learned that a single disease can occur in different people because of several mutated genes. That helps to explain why some treatments work for certain people but not for others.

Even with a rough draft of the human genome sequence completed, much work remains. Scientists will need to figure out what the chains of letters in the genome sequence are trying to say. We need to find ways of understanding the human genome and using that information to improve life for the whole species. In the next chapter, we'll examine what this might mean.

KEY QUESTIONS

* **Why do you think one group made its findings available to the public for free and another kept its discoveries secret? What were their different goals?**

* **Why do you think scientists are using today's gene technology to learn about the past? What can we use this knowledge for?**

HOW BIG IS YOUR GENOME?

Every living thing has a set of instructions stored in its DNA. With only four nucleotide bases (A, T, C, and G), DNA builds a code that is unique for every organism. An organism's entire DNA code is its genome. The size of a genome is different for every species and its mass is measured in picograms (pg). A picogram is a very small, microscopic measurement. One picogram equals 1 trillionth of a gram. The size of a genome in picograms is called its C-value. This number is used to compare the genome size of one species to another. In this activity, you will use an online database to compare the sizes of genomes for several species.

- **To start, predict the genome sizes of the following species by putting them in order from smallest to largest genome:** giraffe, human, cape golden mole, gecko, ghost spider, softshell clam, and centipede.

- **Using the Animal Genome Size Database, look up the C-value for each animal.** You can find the database here.

  > Animal Genome Size Database

- **Prepare a chart to organize your data.** What did you find out? Which animal had the largest genome? Which had the smallest? How accurate was your prediction?

- **Do you think there is a relationship between genome size and organism complexity?** Why or why not?

To investigate more, try comparing the genome sizes of other organisms—plants, fungi, protists, bacteria, and archaebacteria. How do they compare to each other and to humans?

Chapter 3 ▶

What Does the Human Genome Tell Us?

Why is it important to apply scientific discoveries to real-world problems?

Although scientific inquiry is a noble pursuit on its own, when the knowledge gained through the field can be applied to goals such as curing diseases, the entire human race benefits.

The completion of the Human Genome Project was just the beginning of genomic study. As with so many things in the realm of science, more questions begged to be answered. Although we knew the sequence of bases in the human genome, what did it mean? What can the human genome tell us? How does it compare to other genomes? How can the HGP make a difference in our lives?

It always feels good to reach a goal, right? But there's more to reaching a goal than the feeling of satisfaction. A good scientist considers what use their discoveries can be to the human race, to the environment, and to other species. The impact of the HGP is no different.

Even after the monumental achievement of completing the HGP, there was more to be done.

Once the HGP provided the sequence of nucleotide bases in the human genome, the next step was to interpret it so we could understand what it all means. A process called gene annotation takes the raw DNA sequence and identifies the locations of genes and other coding regions in a genome. It also attempts to determine what those genes do.

> In this way, gene annotation takes the genome sequence and tries to make sense of it. It makes the nucleotide sequence meaningful.

Gene annotation involves three main steps.

- First, scientists identify the noncoding regions of the genome. This step is important because it limits the areas of the genome that scientists need to analyze and focuses their efforts on the essential coding sections.

- The next step is identifying elements on the genome, a process called gene prediction. Gene prediction identifies regions that encode genes, such as those that code for proteins and other regions that regulate gene activity.

- Finally, scientists link biological information to these elements.

THE SEARCH FOR GENES

Annotating the human genome is an extremely complicated task! Before the HGP started, scientists estimated the human genome had between 40,000 to 100,000 genes—maybe more. After the project was finished, that estimate dropped to between 20,000 to 25,000 genes.

1000 GENOMES PROJECT

The original HGP sequenced DNA from only a handful of individuals. Launched in 2008, the 1000 Genomes Project sequenced the genomes of more than 2,500 individuals from 26 different populations worldwide. With this information, scientists put together the largest and most detailed catalog of human genetic variation available to date. Medical researchers hope this information will help them identify the genomic variations that are linked to rare and common diseases in people worldwide.

Scientists also discovered that only about 1 percent of human DNA is made up of protein-coding genes. The other 99 percent of the genome is noncoding.

Scientists once believed that noncoding DNA was junk and had no purpose. However, they have learned that some noncoding sequences control gene activity. For example, some noncoding DNA controls where and when genes are turned off and on. Other areas of noncoding DNA hold the instructions to make RNA molecules, which act as messengers carrying instructions from DNA to the cell. At least some noncoding DNA isn't junk at all! We don't know yet what might be revealed about other noncoding DNA.

Even within a single human gene, there are coding and noncoding regions. The human genome consists of small segments of DNA called exons that code for proteins.

Exons are separated by noncoding sequences of DNA called introns.

The lengths of exons and introns vary greatly. A gene may have 10,000 bases, but only about 1,000 bases are actually part of the coding sequence.

A

● A ● B ○ C ○ D ○ F ● G ● H ● I ● J ● K ● L0 ● L1 ○ L2
○ L3 ○ L4 ○ L5 ● M ● N ● R ● T ● U ● V ● W ● X ● Y ● Z

B

Cont	Pop	African						East Asian						Euro-Indian									Asian		American		
		L0	L1	L2	L3	L4	L5	D	F	G	N	Y	Z	H	I	J	K	T	V	W	X	U	M	R	A	B	C
African	ESN	7	20	27	43	2																					
	GWD		15	48	42	2																					
	LWK	18	8	12	47	5	10															6					
	MSL	2	17	39	24	1																2	1				
	YRI	5	17	38	47	1																					
East Asian	CDX							12	25														24	14	19	5	
	CHB							23	16	5	8		1										19	6	7	12	5
	CHS							23	16	2	10		3				1						19	11	6	16	2
	JPT							39	6	11	9	1	4										14		6	14	
	KHV							2	27			4	1										33	11	1	21	1
European	CEU													51	1	8	3	10	3	5		18					
	FIN													37	2	7	6	3	4	2	2	36					
	GBR													39	3	10	5			2	5	18					
	IBS		1		1							2		58	1	4	7	8	6			18		1			
	TSI		1					1						54		8	9	13	2	4	1	15					
Indian	BEB							2	1					1	2							11	58	8	1		
	GIH			1	2									7	1	1	2			2	2	15	41	32			
	ITU											1		2	1	1	4				5	14	61	13			
	PJL								3	2				7	1			3			2	11	55	11			
	STU										3			12	1							14	50	22	1		
Admixed American	ACB	4	21	38	26	1								1	1							1			1	1	1
	ASW	7	16	14	24			1														1	1		1		1
	CLM	1	2	2	4			2						1				2					1		40	33	6
	MXL							9						5					1	1		2			25	15	9
	PEL			1	2			13						1											14	40	15
	PUR	2	5	4	10									2	6	1	1					4			38	7	25
	World	46	123	224	272	12	10	127	94	20	37	2	8	278	8	50	34	56	16	25	11	186	377	129	141	178	70

credit: Lavanya Rishishwar and I. King Jordan (CC BY 4.0 International)

In addition, the distribution of genes on a chromosome is not uniform. Some regions may have a large number of genes, while other regions on a chromosome have far fewer. These are just some of the factors that make identifying genes in the human genome so difficult.

THE ENCODE PROJECT

The HGP produced the sequence of the 3 billion pairs of nucleotide bases in the human genome. The sequence gave scientists a blueprint of the genome. Then, they had to figure out how the blueprint worked.

In September 2003, National Human Genome Research Institute (NHGRI) launched a project named the Encyclopedia of DNA Elements (ENCODE). The goal of ENCODE was to identify and describe all of the functional parts of the human genome. By doing so, scientists hoped to gain insight on how the genome actually worked.

> As with the Human Genome Project, NHGRI committed to sharing ENCODE results with the public.

During the next decade, hundreds of researchers from labs worldwide linked more than 80 percent of the human genome sequence to specific biological functions. They mapped more than 4 million regulatory regions where proteins interacted with DNA. These findings gave them a much better understanding of how proteins turn genes on and off. They realized that the areas of DNA that did not code for a protein were not just junk DNA, but instead played a role as a type of genetic switch.

You can explore the ENCODE catalog at this website. This site is used by scientists and much of it is very advanced, but it's always interesting to see actual applications of the concepts we're talking about in this book!

 ENCODE

GENE GENIUS

It confirmed that the number of genes that coded for proteins was between 20,000 to 25,000. It also identified thousands of other genes that had important roles in cells.

Noncoding DNA turns genes on and off to control when and where proteins are produced.

In September 2012, ENCODE published its results in a catalog of genetic data. The ENCODE catalog is like an operating manual for the human genome.

Scientists have used the data from the ENCODE project in disease research. For example, many regions of the human genome that do not contain protein-coding genes have been associated with disease.

These DNA regions often contain regulatory areas. Instead of affecting the protein itself, genetic changes in these areas may affect how much of a protein is made or when it is made. The disease may occur because abnormal amounts of the protein are being made.

That 0.1 percent variation in your genes is what makes you different!

credit: DoD photo by Elaine Wilson

Identifying the regulatory areas of the human genome can also explain why different types of cells have different properties. Why do muscle cells contract and generate force, while liver cells break down food? Although they both have the same complete set of DNA, muscle cells turn on specific genes, while liver cells turn on other genes.

With more research, investigators hope to better understand how the regulatory regions of DNA may control this process.

TINY DIFFERENCE

Humans come in many sizes and shapes. They have different personalities, skills, and interests. All of these characteristics make each person unique. However, at the genetic level, any two humans are about 99.9 percent identical. On average, the genomes of any two people differ by only one base out of every thousand bases. That tiny, 0.1 percent of variation in your genes makes you different from your brother or your neighbor!

> That 0.1 percent genetic variation also holds the answer to many biological questions.

Why do we look the way we do? Why are some people better at sports while others are better at art? Why do some people develop a disease while others do not? These are just a few of the questions that scientists hope to answer by studying the tiny differences in the human genome.

INTERNATIONAL HAPMAP PROJECT

To better understand variation in the human genome, a group of researchers led by the NIH launched the International HapMap Project in October 2002. The $100-million project included scientists from public agencies and private organizations from around the world. Using the genome sequence provided by the HGP, the project attempted to map common human genome variations using four population groups: the Yoruba from Nigeria, Japanese in Tokyo, Han Chinese in Beijing, and Utah citizens with northern and western European ancestry.

HELPFUL VARIATIONS

Some genetic variations develop because they are a benefit to the survival of an organism. For example, the genetic variation of the beta-globin gene that causes sickle cell disease is more commonly found in people who lived or had ancestors who lived in regions where malaria was common. Malaria is a serious and sometimes fatal disease that resembles the flu. It is caused by a parasite and is often transmitted from one person to another through the bite of a mosquito. People with the sickle cell variation of the beta-globin gene were protected against the malaria infection. In areas where malaria was a deadly killer, having the sickle cell variation was a good thing—you had a better chance of surviving and passing this genetic variation on to your children.

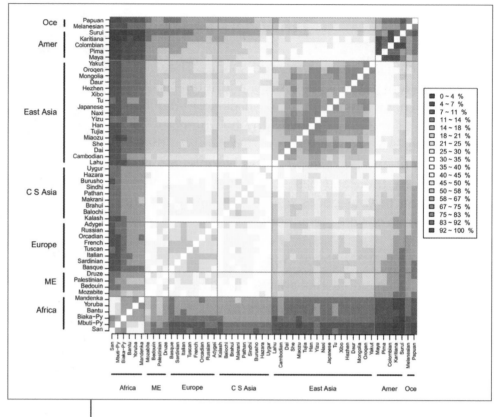

Genetic similarities between 51 worldwide human populations

credit: Tiago R. Magalhães, Jillian P. Casey, Judith Conroy, Regina Regan, Darren J. Fitzpatrick, Naisha Shah, João Sobral, Sean Ennis (CC BY 2.5)

While the Human Genome Project focused on the 99.9 percent of similarities in the human genome, the HapMap project focused on the 0.1 percent of variation.

In the HapMap project, researchers created a catalog of common genetic variations in humans. A genetic variation is the difference in DNA between one person and another. To identify variations, scientists looked for sites in the genome where the DNA sequence was different by a single base—A, C, G, or T. This type of variation is called a single nucleotide polymorphism (SNP) and is the most common type of DNA sequence variation in the human genome.

Most of the time, an SNP does not cause an important biological change in an organism, just as the meaning of a word does not change when a single letter is changed, such as in "realize" and "realise." In some cases, the change of a single base can slightly change the gene's function.

THE HUMAN GENOME | CHAPTER THREE

Other times, it can drastically change a gene's function. Think about how the change in one letter can change a word's meaning, such as "cat" and "sat."

Researchers believe there are about 10 million SNPs in the human genome. Looking for all of these variations would be extremely time consuming and expensive. Luckily, scientists discovered a way to reduce the workload. As part of the HapMap project, researchers discovered that groups of SNPs often cluster in the same areas on chromosomes. These clusters are called haplotypes.

When completed in 2005, the HapMap project created a map of where these haplotype blocks could be found on chromosomes. It described specific variations common in the human genome and where these variations were located on chromosomes.

By comparing the HapMap details of different people, scientists could identify and compare areas of things such as genetic variation between two individuals and learn which of them is more likely to get cancer or which person is more likely to avoid developing dementia. This map made it easier for scientists to search for genetic variations and link a specific gene to a disease.

HOW DO WE COMPARE?

Although the main focus of the HGP was to sequence the human genome to provide a map to learn more about genes and disease, some scientists working on other species—plants, animals, fungi, bacteria, and viruses—are using the knowledge gained from the HPG in their own genomic studies. This has led to a branch of genomic research called comparative genomics.

The HapMap project is also mapping certain common genetic variations in specific populations around the world. This information helps scientists understand more about the disease risks of certain groups of people as well as how the environment has affected the genome.

GENE GENIUS

Researchers have found three key genes involved in inflammation in humans that appear to be absent in the chimpanzee genome. This absence might explain why chimps respond differently to certain illnesses.

Despite their small size, mice and rats have genomes that are about the same size and contain a similar number of genes as humans. The human genome is about 85 percent identical to the rat and mouse genomes. These similarities explain why scientists have found using mice and rats in laboratory studies to be valuable.

Comparative genomics is an area of study in which scientists compare the complete genome sequences of different species.

Why would they want to do that? By comparing the characteristics that define organisms, they can identify similar and different areas in the genomes.

Comparative genomics can also help scientists study evolutionary changes among various organisms. This research can help them identify the genes that are the same among species as well as the genes that are different—those that give each species its unique characteristics.

This fruit fly is about 60 percent genetically identical to humans!

credit: Martin Cooper (CC BY 2.0)

Scientists use high-powered computers to compare the human genome to the genomes of other species. By comparing the DNA sequences in the two genomes, they can determine how closely related humans are to other species.

For example, our closest relative, the chimpanzee, has a genome that is approximately 96 percent identical to the human genome, according to a National Geographic study. That shows how it takes only a tiny percentage of genomic difference to make a large impact.

Scientists can also use comparative genomics to study and understand disease. For example, although the chimpanzee genome is about 96 percent identical to the human genome, chimpanzees do not get certain human diseases, such as malaria and AIDS. Comparing the sequence of genes involved in these diseases might help scientists understand why humans are susceptible to these diseases while chimps are not.

> One day, the insights learned from comparing the two genomes could lead to new ways to treat and prevent these diseases and others.

Funny enough, the genome of the fruit fly is about 60 percent identical to the human genome! These two organisms, which look and behave very differently, share a core set of genes. By comparing the two genomes, researchers have discovered that about two-thirds of the human genes known to be linked to cancer have an equivalent gene in the fruit fly. In addition, when scientists inserted a human gene linked to early-onset Parkinson's disease into fruit flies, the flies showed symptoms similar to those observed in humans with the disease.

MUTANTS!

DNA's sequence of nucleotide bases is the code that carries the instructions for building proteins. While a change in one nucleotide in a long string of DNA may not seem like a big deal, it can have a real effect on an organism. There are three main types of mutation.

- Substitution: One base is substituted for another in a DNA sequence.

- Insertion: An entire base is added to the DNA sequence.

- Deletion: An entire base is removed from the DNA sequence.

Mutations often occur when the cell makes a mistake while copying DNA for cell division. Other times, mutations occur when environmental agents called mutagens damage DNA. Mutagens such as ultraviolet light, radiation, and some chemicals can damage DNA by altering nucleotide bases so they look like other nucleotide bases. When DNA is copied, the damaged base might pair with an incorrect base, causing a mutation. Most of the time, mutations make no noticeable change in a gene's expression function. Other times, a gene mutation causes a serious effect. If the mutation affects the gene's ability to make a critical protein, then the cells that use that protein might not be able to work properly. This is one cause of cancer.

GENE GENIUS

A selective sweep is a mutation that occurs in a population and is so beneficial that it spreads through the population within a few hundred generations and eventually becomes the "normal" sequence. Your skin color is an example of selective sweep in humans. In Africa, our human ancestors had dark skin to protect against the sun's direct ultraviolet rays. As our human ancestors moved from Africa to regions with less direct sunlight, the dark skin pigments were no longer needed for survival. Groups of early humans that moved to Asia and Europe gradually lost their dark pigment and their skin became lighter in color.

Scientists hope that this discovery will one day lead to fruit flies being used as a new model to test treatments for Parkinson's disease.

Comparative genomics may also help scientists better understand Earth's evolutionary tree. Plants, animals, fungi, and bacteria may all look and behave differently, but they are all living creatures with genomes made of DNA, which holds the genes that code for thousands of proteins in each organism.

As the tools for sequencing genomes become more advanced, scientists will be able to compare more and more species, which might lead to discovering unknown connections among the species. Plus, this information could help scientists find new ways to conserve rare and endangered species.

SO MUCH DATA!

How many photos do you have on your phone or other device? Most people have hundreds, if not thousands of pictures! That's a lot of data, and it can be hard to find the one photo you're looking for in a sea of photos you don't want. Scientists have the same problem with their scientific data.

The HGP and the sequencing of other genomes has created a flood of data that scientists need to process, analyze, and store. To do so, they have turned to bioinformatics, a branch of biology that combines computer science, statistics, and math to understand biological processes.

> Bioinformatics uses various computer technologies to better manage and study the vast amounts of biological and genomic data.

It includes databases and knowledge bases to store, recall, and arrange data. Bioinformatics also develops methods and computer software tools to help scientists understand vast amounts of biological and genomic data. Bioinformatics can take enormous data sets and make sense of them.

Using high-powered computers, scientists can gather, compile, manipulate, and analyze large amounts of biological and genomic data. The HGP is one example of how bioinformatics can be used. Remember, the human genome has more than 3 billion base pairs. It's essentially impossible to map all these pairs by hand!

However, using bioinformatics to compile, store, and analyze the data from human genome, scientists have been able to identify genome patterns in disease development. This has led to advances in treatments for different diseases.

We've touched on how different genetic markers can indicate whether or not a person will be more likely to get a disease at some point in their lifetime. In the next chapter, we'll dive deeper into the impact the human genome has on health issues.

TEXT TO WORLD

Look around at your friends and classmates. How are you all different? In what ways are you similar?

KEY QUESTIONS

- Why is data collection and storage such a major part of the Human Genome Project?

- Is there any danger in studying the genetic similarities and differences of different groups of people? Research times in history when people used science to harm instead of help.

Ideas for Supplies

- small jar with lid
- fresh freesia flowers
- PTC strips (used to test taste)
- fresh, chopped coriander
- small mirror
- tissues or wet wipes

INVESTIGATE GENETIC VARIATION

There are a number of physical traits that make every person different. Comparing the genomes of different individuals can identify where differences exist in DNA and the effects these differences have on physical characteristics and health. Understanding these small DNA changes can help improve our knowledge of how the genome works. In this activity, you will investigate some physical characteristics and their variations and consider if they are examples of genetic variation.

- **To start, crush the freesia flowers in a small jar.** Keep the jar sealed until used later in this activity.

- **Test the following characteristics on at least 20 people.** Record your observations in your science journal.

  - Bitter taste: Ask the subject to place a PTC strip on the tip of their tongue. Does it taste bitter or sweet?

  - Coriander taste: What does the person taste when they put a small amount of coriander on their tongue? Does it have an herby taste or a soapy taste?

  - Smell: Open the jar of crushed flowers and ask the subject to sniff. Can they smell anything?

- Earwax type: Use a wet wipe or tissue to gently wipe the entrance to the ear canal. Do not put anything inside the ear! Is there any earwax present? Is it dry or wet and sticky?

- Freckles: Does the subject have freckles?

- Dimples: Does the subject have dimples when they smile?

- Hand clasping: Have the subject clasp their hands together. Do they put their right thumb over the left or the left thumb over the right one?

- **Create a data collection chart to organize your data.**

- **Once you have collected data from at least 20 people, create a bar graph to show the distribution of the different characteristics.** What characteristics do you think are the most linked by genes? Which do you think could be due to other factors, such as education or environment? Choose one of the tested characteristics and research if scientists have linked it to a gene.

To investigate more, explore other characteristics that may be controlled by genes. How can you test for them? Also, try conducting this activity using people from several generations of at least two different families. What do your results tell you about genetic variation and heredity?

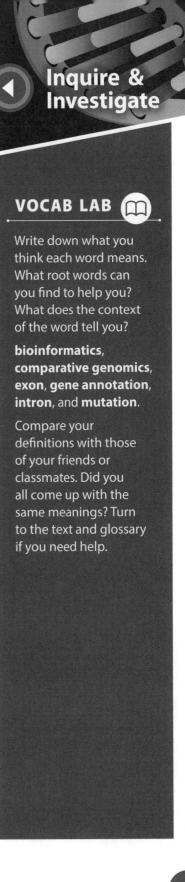

Inquire & Investigate

VOCAB LAB

Write down what you think each word means. What root words can you find to help you? What does the context of the word tell you?

bioinformatics, comparative genomics, exon, gene annotation, intron, and **mutation.**

Compare your definitions with those of your friends or classmates. Did you all come up with the same meanings? Turn to the text and glossary if you need help.

HOW MUTATIONS OCCUR

Some mutations are linked to genetic disorders. Some diseases are linked to a mutation in a single gene, while others are caused by mutations on several genes, helped along with environmental factors. In this activity, you will explore how easily DNA mutations can occur.

- **To start, divide your classmates into groups of at least 10 students.** Have them stand in a single file line. Make sure there is enough space between each person so they cannot hear the instructions given to the person in front of them.

- **Give the first student in each line the same set of instructions.** For example, tell them to draw a series of symbols or perform a series of actions. Make sure the rest of the students in the line do not hear the instructions.

- **Have the first student whisper the instructions to the second student in line.** The second student will whisper to the third student and continue down the line until the last student receives the instructions. How does this model what happens to DNA during several rounds of replication?

- **The last student in line should perform the instructions that they received.** What does this step represent?

- **Have the first student perform the original instructions that they received.** How does this compare to what the last student did? What types of mutations occurred in the instructions between the first and last students? How could these changes in the genome affect human health?

To investigate more, change the set of instructions or change how you deliver the instructions. How does this affect the mutations that arise? Why do you think this occurs?

Chapter 4 ▶
Using the Human Genome to Improve Health

How are genes
used in the field
of health care?

ARE THOSE THE RESULTS OF YOUR GENETIC TEST?

YES, AND IT SAYS THAT I HAVE AN INCREASED CHANCE OF TYPE 2 DIABETES!!

DON'T PANIC! YOU'RE NOT DOOMED!

TYPE 2 DIABETES IS CAUSED BY GENETICS AND ENVIRONMENT.

SO IF YOU EAT HEALTHY AND EXERCISE, YOU MIGHT NEVER EVEN GET IT.

THAT'S A RELIEF! BUT DOES THAT MEAN I HAVE TO STOP EATING ICE CREAM FOR DINNER?

YES, THAT IS EXACTLY WHAT THAT MEANS!

Genetics is an important consideration for health professionals when they examine someone's level of risk, appropriate treatment, and ways to keep people from getting sick in the first place!

Using the human genome sequence as a map, scientists are learning more every day about the relationship between our genome and human health. With this information, they are developing new ways to better diagnose, treat, and prevent human disease.

Even before the Human Genome Project, doctors frequently used genetic testing to identify carriers of certain genetic diseases. Doctors had some tools they could use to screen newborns for genetic disease and diagnose some types of cancer. But many diseases went unidentified until much later in life. Parents who might be carriers of genetic diseases passed on those genes to their babies without knowing the danger.

A genetic disease is an inherited condition caused by an abnormality in a person's DNA—a mutation. As we discussed in the previous chapter, the abnormality can be as small as a change in a single base in one gene or it can involve the addition or subtraction of an entire chromosome.

Many of the diseases that doctors were able to diagnose and test for were single-gene diseases, caused by an abnormality in a single gene. These were simpler to find. With the completed human genome sequence, however, scientists have been able to greatly improve their ability to identify and diagnose many more conditions.

Since the complete sequencing of the human genome, scientists have discovered more than 1,800 disease genes! Plus, it now takes far less time to find a disease gene. Today's scientists can find a gene suspected of causing a genetic disease in days, rather than the years it took before they had the human genome sequence as a tool.

As a result, there are now more than 2,000 genetic tests for human diseases. These tests allow patients to learn their own risk for genetic disease, while also helping doctors diagnose disease in patients.

CASE STUDY: A RARE GENETIC DISEASE

Some diseases are so rare, you might not have heard of them before. Progeria is an extremely rare genetic disease of childhood that causes dramatic, premature aging. The disease affects approximately one in 4 million infants worldwide.

The most severe form of progeria is called Hutchinson-Gilford progeria syndrome, named after the doctors who first described the disease in 1886 and 1904.

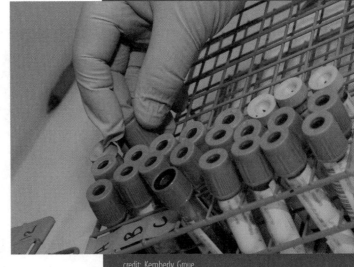

credit: Kemberly Groue

Children with progeria appear normal at birth. Within a year, though, their growth rate slows—they are shorter and weigh less than other children of the same age. Their appearance resembles that of an old person with baldness, wrinkled skin, pinched nose, and a small face and jaw relative to head size.

Children with progeria often suffer from symptoms of old age, such as joint stiffness, hip dislocations, and cardiovascular disease. To date, there is no cure for progeria. Children with it die on average at age 13, often from a heart attack or stroke.

In 2003, a team of researchers with the National Human Genome Research Institute, the Progeria Research Foundation, and other organizations discovered the gene that causes Hutchinson-Gilford progeria. The disease is caused by a tiny, point mutation in a single gene called lamin A (LMNA), located on chromosome 1.

A point mutation occurs when a single nucleotide base is changed, inserted, or deleted from a sequence of DNA. The LMNA gene consists of 25,000 base pairs and the substitution of a single pair causes the devastating disease.

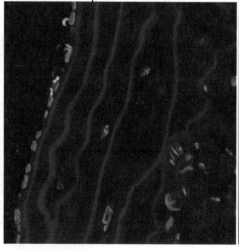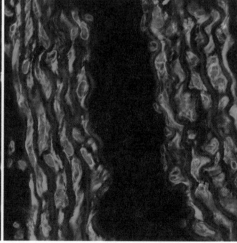

Progeria in mice—the left side are cells left untreated, while the right side are cells treated with a certain medication.

Why does this tiny change among thousands of bases matter? The LMNA gene codes for two proteins in humans, lamin A and lamin C. Both proteins have important roles in stabilizing the inner membrane of a cell's nucleus. At first, such a small change would seem to have little effect on the gene and its production of lamin A protein. However, when testing cells from progeria patients, researchers found that the mutation in the LMNA gene causes the cell to produce an abnormal form of lamin A.

This abnormal protein changes the cell's nuclear membrane, which can be especially harmful to cells and tissues in the cardiovascular and musculoskeletal systems. This finding could explain why the disease causes problems with organs and structures in these systems, such as the heart, muscles, and skeleton.

Researchers also noted that the parents and siblings of children with progeria were almost never affected by the disease. That led them to believe that the genetic abnormality was not hereditary. Instead, they found evidence that the genetic mutation occurs in the male sperm before the baby is even conceived.

With these breakthroughs, scientists developed a genetic test for Hutchinson-Gilford progeria syndrome. Before this genetic test, doctors used a patient's physical symptoms to diagnose progeria. But these symptoms usually did not even appear until a child was a few years old. With a genetic test, doctors can diagnose the disease much earlier, which allows them to start treatment earlier.

Although there is currently no cure for progeria, scientists hope that as they learn more about the genetic causes of progeria, they will be able to develop better treatments and eventually find a cure.

GENE GENIUS

People with mutations in genes that increase risk of colon cancer benefit from earlier and more frequent screening for colon cancer.

Doctors at NIH working on cutting-edge genetic science.

TYPE 2 DIABETES

At first, the pancreas makes extra insulin to keep blood glucose at a normal level. As time passes, the pancreas continues to make too much insulin, but the body cannot use it efficiently. As a result, blood glucose becomes too high. When glucose builds up in the blood, the body's cells lack the energy they need. High blood glucose levels can cause damage to a person's eyes, kidneys, nerves, and heart.

A GANG OF GENES

While some diseases are caused by a single change in a gene, many more are linked to changes in multiple genes spread out across the human genome.

Some diseases are caused by a combination of genes acting together along with environmental factors. These diseases are called polygenic disorders. Using the map provided by the HGP, scientists are working to get a better understanding of how multiple genes interact with each other and the environment to cause human disease.

Do you or anyone you know have diabetes? Many people all around the world suffer from diabetes, a group of diseases that causes too much sugar to form in the blood. Diabetes is an example of a polygenic disorder.

One of the most common forms of the disease is Type 2 diabetes, a chronic condition that affects the way the body processes blood sugar. Blood sugar, also called blood glucose, is the body's main source of energy. It comes from the food you eat. An organ in your digestive system called the pancreas produces insulin, a hormone that helps the body process glucose and turn it into energy for cells. In Type 2 diabetes, the body does not use insulin properly and too much glucose builds up in the blood.

Scientists have known that diabetes tends to run in families, which suggests there is a genetic factor that causes the disease. Scientists managed to identify more than 80 tiny DNA differences that appear to raise the risk of Type 2 diabetes in some people or protect others from the disease. Still, no single gene or combination of genes has been identified as causing Type 2 diabetes.

Environmental factors can influence whether or not genetics has an affect on someone's health.

In 2017, a team of researchers made a potential breakthrough. They discovered that many of the changes across the genome in people with Type 2 diabetes affected the same DNA-reading molecule. The molecule, called Regulatory Factor X (RFX), is a regulator for many genes, which means that it controls when the gene turns on and off. Many of the DNA changes linked to Type 2 diabetes affected RFX's ability to read certain sections of DNA in pancreas cells.

The researchers suspect that the DNA changes caused RFX to fail to read DNA's genetic instructions properly, which affected the cell's ability to use insulin effectively to regulate blood sugar. This discovery could explain how multiple changes in genes could cause the same disease.

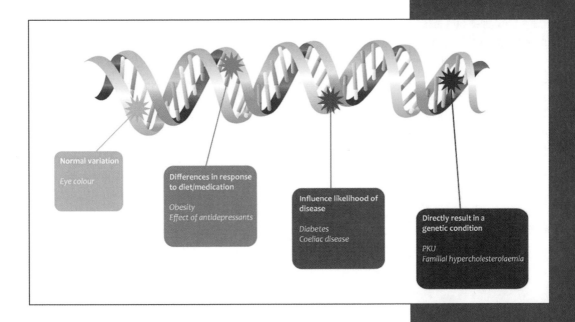

Normal variation

Eye colour

Differences in response to diet/medication

Obesity
Effect of antidepressants

Influence likelihood of disease

Diabetes
Coeliac disease

Directly result in a genetic condition

PKU
Familial hypercholesterolaemia

BLOOD TESTS TO DETECT CANCER

Some cancers are difficult to study because it is hard to get a tissue sample without painful surgery. As an alternative, some scientists are working on a blood test that would detect circulating tumor DNA (ctDNA) instead of taking a tumor tissue sample. As cancer cells grow and die, they release some of their DNA into a patient's blood. New tests are sensitive enough to detect and sequence ctDNA in the blood separately from the patient's normal DNA. This type of test is called a liquid biopsy. It's far easier and less painful than surgery. Although the tests' use is not yet widespread, scientists hope that liquid biopsies will eventually become part of routine cancer detection and care.

This error is like having an oven temperature gauge that cannot measure the oven's temperature correctly. The malfunction then affects the oven's ability to cook food properly.

The vast majority of human diseases are like diabetes—polygenic. Diseases such as asthma, autism, cardiovascular disease, schizophrenia, inflammatory bowel disease, and certain autoimmune disorders are examples of polygenic disorders. Scientists hope that the insights learned by studying the human genome will lead to better ways to diagnose and treat these diseases.

TREATING CANCER

Did you know that because of what we have learned about the human genome, doctors are developing ways to detect cancer with a blood test? Some cancers are even being treated not by where they are in the body, but by the changes in the genomes. Advances in genomic science and DNA sequencing are leading the way to a new understanding of cancer, how it develops, and how to treat it.

> Cancer is a group of diseases that result from changes in the genome of cells in the body.

These changes involve DNA mutations that lead the cells to grow uncontrollably. As we discussed earlier, mutations regularly occur in the body, but typically our cells find and fix the mutations as the cells divide and replicate. In some rare cases, however, some mutations escape the cells' repair. These mutations can develop into cancer.

Because of the HGP, scientists know what a healthy human genome looks like. They can use this to identify changes in the genome that lead to cancer. Some projects, such as the Cancer Genome Atlas, have sequenced the genomes of thousands of cancer samples. These projects show that some cancers have mutations in the same group of genes, even if they developed in different tissues.

Many of the mutations activate genes that either promote cell growth or turn off genes that prevent cell growth. This might explain the uncontrolled cell growth seen in cancer.

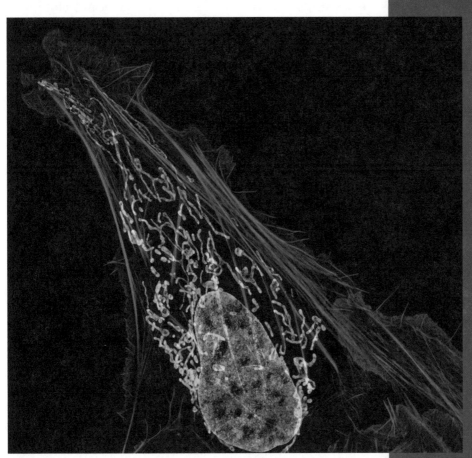

This image shows a cancer cell with DNA in blue, mitochondria in yellow, and actin filaments in purple.

credit: Dylan Burnette and Jennifer Lippincott-Schwartz, Eunice Kennedy Shriver National Institute of Child Health and Human Development, National Institutes of Health

NOT THE SAME

Not all cancer cells are the same, even in the same person! Genome sequencing of cancer cells has revealed that a single patient's cancer cells may carry different combinations of mutations. This might explain why some patients do not respond well to treatment. In one example, doctors had long believed that leukemia was a relatively simple cancer that involved just one type of variation in the cancer's genome, called a subclone. However, in one case, a woman with leukemia was found to have four different subclones. Traditional chemotherapy treatment destroyed cancer cells with three of the four subclones. The final subclone survived. It developed new mutations and caused the patient to relapse. Understanding the different mutations in cancer may one day help doctors determine the right combination of drugs and treatments to kill all subclones.

Scientists hope that by learning about the specific mutations that lead to a patient's cancer, they will be able to design more effective treatments that target the source of the cancer.

CANCER GENOME TO CANCER TREATMENT

As scientists learn more about the genome changes that cause cancers, doctors are exploring how to use this information to better treat patients. In 2003, Dr. Lukas Wartman was a fourth-year medical student when he was first diagnosed with a type of blood cancer called acute lymphoblastic leukemia (ALL). He immediately entered treatment with aggressive chemotherapy, which drove his leukemia into remission.

He graduated from medical school and started his career as a doctor and medical researcher. Wartman's experience as a cancer patient led him to specialize in treating patients with leukemia and studying the disease in his laboratory at Washington University in St. Louis, Missouri.

Five years later, Wartman relapsed—his cancer had returned. At the time, researchers at his university were sequencing cancer genomes. They asked Wartman if they could study him and his cancer. The researchers sequenced the DNA in Wartman's normal cells and compared it to the DNA sequence in his cancerous blood cells.

They found a mutation in the cancer's genome in a gene called FLT3.

The researchers also identified a medication, already approved by the U.S. Food and Drug Administration (FDA) for treating other types of cancer, that had been used to treat patients with mutations in this same gene. Wartman started taking the medicine on a Friday. By Monday, his blood counts had improved.

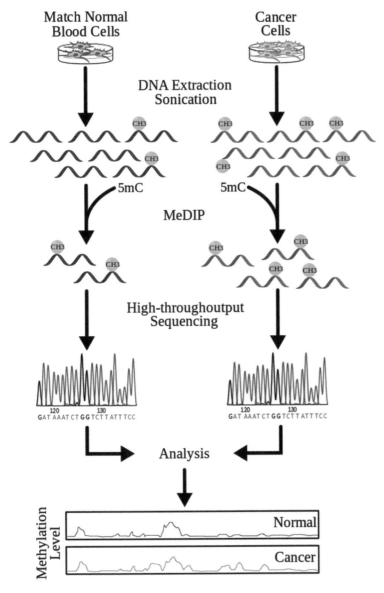

Researchers can pinpoint where cancer mutations occur and target those areas for treatment.

Some common genetic diseases include cystic fibrosis, an inherited, life-threatening disorder that damages the lungs and digestive system, and Huntington's disease, a condition in which nerve cells in the brain break down as a person ages.

GENE GENIUS

Some environmental factors can have an effect on the genome, changing genes and health. For example, identical twins are born with identical genomes, but as their lives go on, one twin is healthier and even lives longer than the other. Why? Because of the impact of the environment on their genetic makeup.

After several weeks, doctors could no longer detect leukemia cells in his blood. This meant that his leukemia had gone into remission. Although he would still need more treatment to make sure the cancer did not come back, Wartman believes that the insights into his cancer that genome sequencing provided saved his life.

MEDICINE JUST FOR YOU

Every person responds to diseases and treatments differently. What if there was a way to personalize your medical treatment to match your body's unique genetic makeup? That's the goal of genomic medicine.

Since the completion of the HGP in 2003, scientists have worked hard to figure out how each of our 20,000 to 25,000 genes functions and how it interacts with every other gene. With genomic medicine, doctors will be able to use a person's DNA to determine the best possible treatment for them.

Small variations in specific genes may make one person more likely to develop a disease while a different variation may protect another person from that disease. Genetic variations may explain why one treatment works well for one person but not at all for another person.

Genomic Medicine Cycle

- Genomics in the Clinic
- Patients and Families
- Description of Disease
- Identification of Genes
- Targeting Specific Genes

As scientists learn more about how small gene differences affect health, they can develop better ways to prevent, diagnose, and treat many diseases and disorders. That's what scientists hope genomic medicine can do.

It's still early times in genomic medicine research! But it has shown promise in several areas. One area is improved screening and diagnostic testing.

In the United States, a public health program called newborn screening tests all babies at birth for up to 50 severe, inherited, and treatable genetic diseases. Through genomic medicine, doctors may one day be able to easily use whole genome sequencing at birth to screen all babies for a larger number of diseases and conditions.

Plus, rapid whole genome sequencing is being used for some very sick babies in hospitals. Because newborns are often difficult to diagnose, doctors can use rapid whole genome sequencing to get a genetic diagnosis within 50 hours. In many cases, the quick diagnosis helps doctors make time-sensitive treatment decisions that improve the newborn's health outcomes.

Genomic medicine can also help doctors design more effective treatments for patients. Colorectal cancer is a type of cancer that forms in the colon (large intestine) or rectum. Low-dose aspirin therapy is often prescribed for patients with colorectal cancer to reduce inflammation. However, its effectiveness varies by patient.

Now, doctors may be able to use genomic medicine to determine which patients will benefit the most from aspirin therapy.

THE CANCER GENOME ATLAS

The Cancer Genome Atlas (TCGA) is a program at the National Institutes of Health to catalog the genomes of thousands of cancer tumors. The tumors span more than 20 different types of cancer, including brain, lung, colon, and breast cancer. The information gathered by this program is advancing the study and treatment of cancer. For example, TCGA data identified a mutation behind a certain kind of lung cancer and a treatment is being developed to target the affected genes. In another example, researchers have found that 68 of the tumor genes in ovarian cancers respond to existing anti-cancer drugs, opening up more effective treatments for this type of cancer. By understanding the genomic changes that drive cancer cell growth, scientists are working to find ways to treat and cure all types of cancer. And by making the information about the genetic makeup of cancer tumors accessible to everyone, they are speeding up the identification process and helping more people every year.

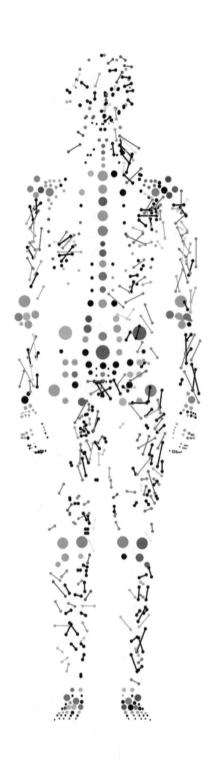

A study by researchers at the Dana-Farber Cancer Institute found that aspirin therapy can extend the life of colorectal cancer patients whose cancer has a particular mutation in the PIK3CA gene. In their study, 97 percent of patients who had the PIK3CA gene mutation and were treated with aspirin therapy were alive five years after diagnosis. That's compared to 74 percent of those with the gene mutation who did not use aspirin. At the same time, aspirin therapy had no effect on the five-year survival rates for patients who did not have the PIK3CA mutation.

> Instead of simply prescribing a treatment to everyone that will only work for some, doctors can begin to prescribe only treatments that have a very good chance of working.

Genomic medicine may one day use genetic information to better treat people who are at risk for certain genetic diseases. This is already happening in some areas. For example, genetic tests can identify people with a high risk of certain cancers, such as women who carry the BRCA gene mutations and have a high risk of developing breast cancer. Knowing this genetic risk allows a woman and her doctor to decide on specific tests and treatments to reduce her risk of cancer.

Other genetic tests can identify breast cancer patients who are most likely to benefit from a drug called Herceptin. Genetic testing can also determine the best dose of a drug called mercaptopurine, which is used to treat leukemia and certain autoimmune diseases, so that the patient avoids severe side effects.

THE PROMISE OF PHARMACOGENOMICS

Have you ever experienced side effects from medication? Drugs affect different people in different ways. One person may find a drug very effective and easy to take, while another patient experiences severe side effects. Now, a new area of genomic medicine called pharmacogenomics is looking to use a person's genome to improve drug treatment and reduce the negative side effects.

Personalized medicine is a pretty new way of treating patients. Learn more about it in this video. Can you think of any drawbacks to pharmacogenetics?

 Megan Ensinger pharmacogenomics

GENETIC RISK FOR BREAST CANCER

For most women, the risk of developing breast cancer in their lifetime is small. They undergo routine breast exams and mammogram scans to catch any sign of cancer early. For women who have specific genetic mutations, the risk of developing breast cancer is much higher. Because they carry such a high genetic risk, these women may choose drastic preventive measures, such as surgery to remove their breasts or ovaries or using more advanced magnetic resonance imaging for their screenings.

The field of pharmacogenomics studies how a person's genes affect the way they respond to drugs. Researchers hope that, using genomics, they will be able to personalize what drugs and doses are prescribed to each patient for the best outcomes.

Imagine that you have high blood pressure. Before prescribing medication, your doctor sequences your genome. They might find a variation in your genome that means a commonly used drug to treat high blood pressure would have little effect on you and might increase your risk of heart attack. Your doctor would not prescribe that medication for you. Instead, they would prescribe another drug to reduce your blood pressure without negative side effects.

This type of scenario is already happening in real life. Abacavir is a commonly prescribed drug for HIV, the virus that causes AIDS. When some patients used the drug, they developed rashes, fatigue, and diarrhea. All of these complaints are symptoms of a potential immune system reaction. Scientists have identified a genome variation associated with the immune system that causes these reactions. Now, doctors test for this genome variation before they prescribe the drug. Patients have a better chance of staying well.

SO, HOW'S YOUR GENOME?

To learn more about disease, scientists compare the genomes of people with a disease to those without the illness. This comparison, called a genome-wide association study (GWAS), enables scientists to more easily identify the differences in genomes between sick and healthy people. With this information, researchers can develop new targets for therapies to treat and even prevent the disease.

Early on, the work of genomic association was slow and tedious. It was hard for researchers to identify which genes were involved in disease and find where they were located in the human genome. With the HapMap project and other technological advances in genomic science, researchers now have powerful tools to help them more quickly find the variations in DNA linked to a disease. With this information, they can predict whether a certain mutation is associated with a specific disease—eventually, they'll be able to identify people at risk.

For example, researchers in the United Kingdom compared the genomes of 2,000 people who had one of seven common disorders. They compared those genomes to 3,000 healthy people. This comparison enabled researchers to identify new genetic markers associated with an increased risk for heart disease and diabetes. With this type of information, scientists can determine a person's risk of developing a disease based on the markers in their individual genome.

We live in a very interesting present, and the future looks bright in terms of genomic health! But what about the past? Can the map of the human genome help us understand where we came from and how we developed? We'll take a journey back in time in the next chapter.

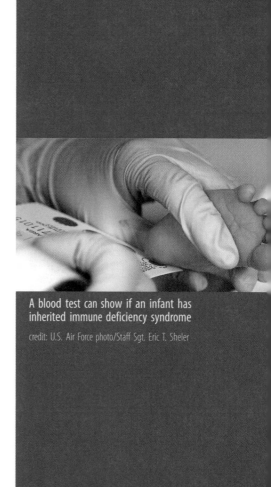

A blood test can show if an infant has inherited immune deficiency syndrome

credit: U.S. Air Force photo/Staff Sgt. Eric T. Sheler

KEY QUESTIONS

- **Why might certain diseases get more attention from researchers studying genomics than other diseases?**
- **Personalized medicine used to be the stuff of science fiction! What other inventions that now appear in fiction might someday be fact?**

TEXT TO WORLD

Some people debate who should receive very expensive medical treatment. Should age, income, or location matter? Why or why not?

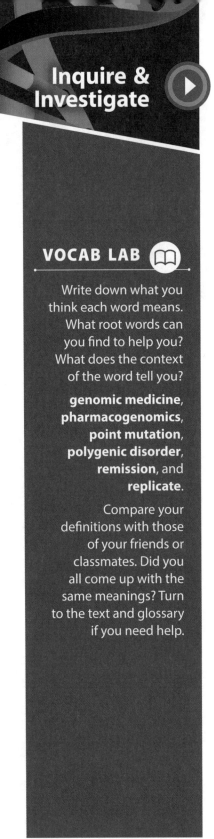

VOCAB LAB

Write down what you think each word means. What root words can you find to help you? What does the context of the word tell you?

genomic medicine, **pharmacogenomics**, **point mutation**, **polygenic disorder**, **remission**, and **replicate**.

Compare your definitions with those of your friends or classmates. Did you all come up with the same meanings? Turn to the text and glossary if you need help.

PHARMACOGENOMICS: HOW THE GENOME AFFECTS DRUG RESPONSE

Prescription drugs save lives around the world. They help prevent heart attacks and treat different types of cancer. However, not everyone has the same response to the same medication. Different responses to a medication are often caused by differences in the genome. A single DNA mutation in a person's genome can be associated with an increased or decreased response to a particular medication.

When pharmaceutical companies develop a new drug, they test it on many people to see if any have different responses to the drug. They can then do a genetic screening to see if the people who had a different response have a mutation that the others do not have, or a single nucleotide polymorphism (SNP).

Once SNPs that are associated with an abnormal response to the drug are identified, doctors can screen patients for these SNPs so they will know how a patient will respond to the drug before they prescribe it. In this activity, you will choose a common drug and investigate how a genetic mutation is associated with a person's response to this drug and how the mutation affects the way the body processes the drug.

* **To start, choose a common drug to study.** Some drugs have large amounts of data available.

  * Azathioprine (Imuran) – treats rheumatoid arthritis

 NCBI NBK100661

- Celecoxib (Celebrex) – treats arthritis   NCBI NBK379478

- Clopidogrel (Plavix) – prevents blood clots   NCBI NBK84114

- Mercaptopurine (Purinethol) – treats leukemia NCBI NBK100660

- Warfarin (Coumadin) – prevents blood clots   NCBI NBK84174

- **Learn about the medication.** What conditions does it treat? What types of patients would use this drug? How does the drug affect the body? What pathways does it use?

- **What changes in a person's genome can affect how they react to this drug?** How does this affect the treatment of their disease? How can doctors use this information to make treatment decisions?

> To investigate more, consider that pharmacogenomic information is currently being used to prescribe medications for only a few conditions. What other diseases and disorders could benefit from using pharmacogenomic information to find better ways of using medications? Why?

CREATE A PERSONALIZED MEDICINE BROCHURE

Personalized medicine has great potential to improve human health. As genome research improves and the cost of genome analysis decreases, the opportunities to use information from a person's genome to drive their health care decisions will increase. Here are some of the exciting possibilities.

• Using personal genome sequencing to diagnose patients with rare conditions

• Predicting a person's risk of developing a medical condition

• Prescribing medications based on a patient's genome

• Developing new drugs to treat diseases linked to specific genetic variants.

• **In this activity, you will prepare a brochure that highlights the possibilities, breakthroughs, and limits of personalized medicine.** The brochure will be read by the people who may benefit from personalized medicine but may be unaware of the advances in this field. The brochure should include an overview of personalized medicine. It should also present examples of success stories, along with discussing potential challenges. Choose from one of three subtopics to focus on in the brochure.

1. Genetic testing applied to rare disease to diagnose and/or develop a treatment plan

2. Using genetic testing to decide which drug and what dose to prescribe to a patient

3. Developing or prescribing drugs for diseases such as cancer that are targeted to the genetic makeup of specific patients

- **Research the field of personalized medicine to gather information that you will use in the brochure.** There are many news articles available on the internet about personalized medicine that you can read. The brochure should address the following questions.

  - Why are doctors and patients optimistic about personalized medicine?

  - How has personalized medicine helped patients already?

  - How might personalized medicine help people with cystic fibrosis, cancer, or an undiagnosed disease?

  - What are the challenges of personalizing medicine to individuals or small numbers of people?

  - How will personalized medicine affect health care costs?

  - What can we do to ensure access to personalized medicine is fair and equitable?

- **Use markers and colored pencils or a computer to complete the brochure.** Be creative!

To investigate more, choose one of the subtopics that you did not use and create a PowerPoint presentation to share information about the subject with others. Who is your audience? What information will be important to them and should be included in the presentation?

SPOT A CANCER MUTATION

All cancers develop because of changes in the DNA sequence of our genome. These changes cause healthy cells to divide uncontrollably. This happens when the DNA change affects the activity of genes that normally stop cell growth or by turning on genes that control cell division. The result is a mass of cells—a tumor—that continues to grow. In this activity, you will compare DNA sequencing of a healthy cell and a tumor cell.

- **Below are results of DNA sequencing for part of the DNA in a healthy cell and a tumor cell.** Using this key, write the DNA sequence for each sample.

KEY

C G T A

HEALTHY CELL DNA

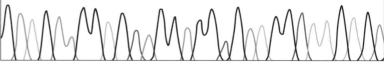

TUMOR CELL DNA

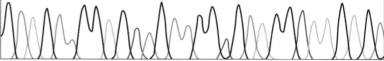

- **Compare the healthy sequence to the tumor sequence.** Is there a difference? If so, circle it.

- **Does this mutation change the amino acid the DNA codes for?** Use the Universal Genetic code to determine what amino acid the healthy sequence codes. (Remember that U – uracil represents T – thymine in the chart) What amino acid does the tumor sequence code for?

- **Why does this mutation matter?** How do you think it contributes to the development of the cancer tumor?

To investigate more, think about how understanding where this mutation occurs in a cancer tumor and what it does helps scientists develop more effective treatments for cancer.

Chapter 5

Human Evolution: The Story of Us

How does studying the human genome teach us about the ancient past?

By studying gene patterns from ancient samples, scientists can follow the path of human migration and relationships from millions of years ago!

Where does the human species come from? How are we all related? From our earliest days, humans have tried to answer these questions. Nearly every society and religion throughout history has a creation story that tells the tale of how we humans came to live on Earth. Now, the information found in the human genome gives us a new way to explain our human history—a record of our evolution captured in our genome.

Your genome reveals clues about the history of your ancestors, both recent and ancient. Advances in DNA sequencing and genomic tools allow scientists to compare genome sequences among humans—both those alive today and those who lived long ago.

With this information, scientists can trace the evolutionary history of the human species. Plus, comparing genomic sequences of people from different populations can reveal the genomic changes that have occurred in those populations as time has passed.

Genomics can help us fill in the story of the human species. Small genomic changes passed down from generation to generation are the link to our ancient ancestors. The story of our species is written in our DNA. Let's take a look.

HELLO, ANCESTORS!

Human evolution is the process of change during a long period of time by which modern humans descended from our ancestors. Evolution does not change any one individual. Instead, it changes the inherited traits in a population. You look and behave differently from early human ancestors because of how the entire human species adapted as a whole.

Some traits are favorable, meaning that they give an organism a survival advantage over other organisms. Organisms that survive are more likely to reproduce and give their genes to their offspring. As generations pass, favorable genetic traits become common in a population.

For example, early humans who were able to outrun predators were less likely to be eaten and more likely to survive and pass on those speedy running skills. These genetic changes in a population can affect what a species eats, how it grows, and where it lives.

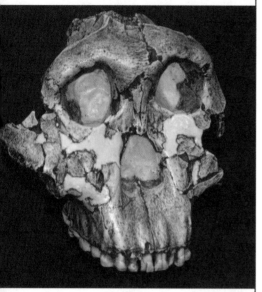

Paranthropus boisei fossil hominid skull found in eastern Africa

credit: James St. John (CC BY 2.0)

GENE GENIUS

In 2015, ancient DNA confirmed that Kennewick Man, an 8,000-year-old skeleton found in Washington state in 1996, was genetically closest to Native Americans.

Humans evolved as new genetic variations in early populations favored traits that allowed them to adapt to the changing environment.

For many years, scientists have used evidence such as early human fossils and other archaeological remains to reconstruct the history of humans on Earth. These fossils include bones, tools, footprints, and other evidence of activity left by early people.

Fossilized bones give scientists information about what early humans looked like and how their appearance changed with time. The size of the bones, their shapes, and markings on the bones from muscles tell scientists how early humans moved and how they held tools. Changing skull sizes illustrate how the size of the human brain has changed. These clues help paint a portrait of what humans, and life in ancient times, was like.

Although fossils and other archaeological evidence are important in learning the history of human evolution, information from the human genome can shed new light on how early humans migrated around the world. It can help illuminate their connections to other species.

ANCIENT DNA TELLS A STORY

Today, scientists have developed a way to extract small amounts of DNA from ancient fossils, such as bones, fur, or soil. A new field of paleogenetics has emerged to study the past through preserved genetic material found in the remains of ancient organisms.

At first, scientists could read only short segments of ancient genomes because the samples they found were incomplete or damaged and they had no reference genome. As a result, they focused their research on particular genes or narrow regions of DNA, such as the male Y-chromosome or mitochondrial DNA inherited from a mother.

However, these short sequences did not tell the full story of human ancestry. To learn more, scientists needed to be able to sequence an entire genome. Although scientists could now sequence the genome from a living human, tackling an entire ancient genome is a challenge. Ancient DNA is very fragile and can easily fall apart. It can also undergo chemical reactions that change its nucleotide code. In addition, ancient DNA samples are often contaminated with DNA from other organisms.

However, technological advances now allow scientists to read billions of bases from the genomes of ancient humans and other organisms. Here's how. To extract ancient DNA, scientists clean ancient bones and other surviving tissue in a sterile lab. They crush a part of the bone into powder and dissolve it with chemicals that isolate short DNA strands. The extract becomes a soup of DNA, some from the ancient sample and other material, such as DNA from microbes that lived in the soil surrounding the remains.

After scientists amplify and sequence the ancient DNA, they use certain clues to authenticate it, or make sure it's a valid sequence. For example, ancient DNA strands are usually shorter than 100 letters. If they find a fragment that is longer, they discard it as a contaminant. Then, scientists use computers to arrange the short strands based on overlapping stretches of code and compare the DNA sequence to other, previously sequenced reference genomes.

CREATING A PORTRAIT OF THE PAST

The Denisovans are a recently discovered group of ancient humans who lived alongside Neanderthals and *Homo sapiens*. To date, only a few fossils have been found of this mysterious group, including a few teeth, a finger bone, and a partial jaw. Even without a complete skull, scientists have been able to reconstruct the face of a young female Denisovan using ancient DNA. The scientists used a technique that allowed them to reconstruct gene activity patterns in the ancient DNA and compare it to the way genes work in different human groups. The way genes activate and express themselves determines the anatomical or physical traits those genes produce. Using this information, scientists recreated the likeness of the ancient female. One day, scientists may be able to use methods like this to produce an entire gallery of ancient human portraits.

Studying ancient human DNA reveals more information than can be learned from fossils or artifacts. It has answered questions—such as whether or not our human ancestors interacted with Neanderthals. According to the DNA, the answer is yes. Ancient genomes show that not only did our ancestors (*Homo sapiens*) meet a similar species, Neanderthals (*Homo neanderthalensis*), but they also produced offspring with them between 40,000 and 100,000 years ago. Today, there are still traces of Neanderthal DNA sequences in our genomes.

> These small areas of DNA may be responsible for traits that helped our ancestors survive, which made it more likely those traits would be passed on to future generations.

As scientists find better ways to extract and isolate ancient DNA and improve DNA sequencing technologies, we will learn more about human history. Ancient DNA studies that span 500,000 years and hundreds of remains are already adding to our knowledge of human history and evolution. Because ancient DNA can be used to track the evolution of diseases and how humans respond to them, the data is even useful for medical research.

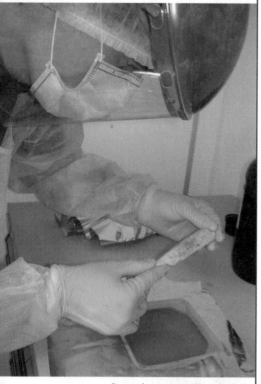

Researchers extract Neanderthal DNA from a sample.

credit: Max Planck Institute for Evolutionary Anthropology

GENE GENIUS

Most ancient DNA has come from fossils younger than 50,000 years and from cold climates.

DECOMPOSING DNA

When an organism dies, its DNA decomposes. How long it takes DNA to decompose depends on a variety of factors, such as temperature, burial conditions, and the number of microbes feasting on the remains. This means the amount of ancient DNA that scientists can study is limited by how well it is preserved.

Scientists predict that in ideal conditions—particularly very cold ones—ancient DNA could survive about 1 million years.

From human-like species, the oldest DNA fragment recovered is from a Neanderthal species and is estimated to be about 430,000 years old. Scientists discovered the Neanderthal remains in a cave in Spain that stays a cool 50 degrees Fahrenheit (10 degrees Celsius) year-round.

Scientists are starting to have success extracting ancient DNA from fossils found in warmer places. This is especially important because human evolution is believed to have started in Africa, which has a hot climate. Researchers have discovered that DNA in petrous bone is preserved better than DNA in other bones. From this tiny, dense bone on the skull, scientists have been able to recover ancient DNA from fossils found in the Middle East that are estimated to be up to 12,000 years old.

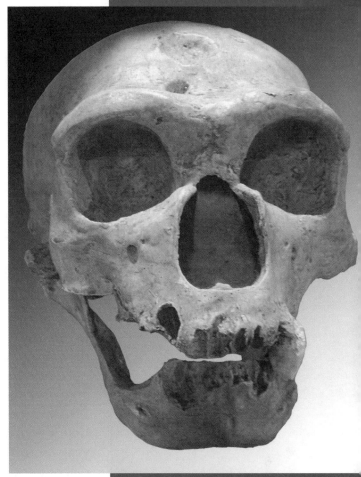

A Neanderthal skull discovered in France in 1908
credit: Luna04 (CC BY 2.0)

FOLLOW THE PATH

Africa has long been known as the "cradle of humanity." Our earliest human ancestors originated on the continent. Using genome sequencing, scientists have been able to follow the path of human migration around the world. When early humans first left Africa around 60,000 years ago, they left genetic footprints that can still be seen today.

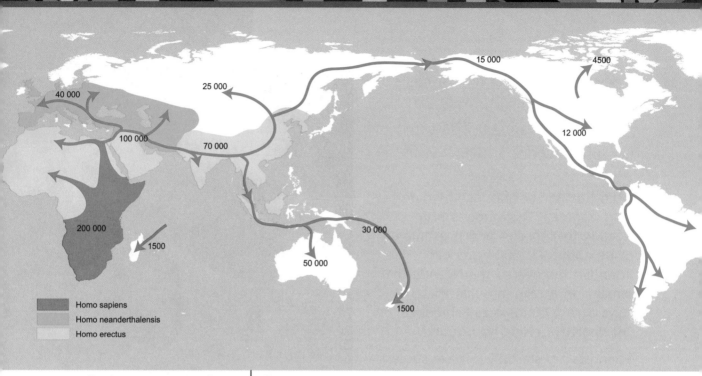

Homo sapiens
Homo neanderthalensis
Homo erectus

How human ancestors spread across the globe from Africa. The numbers show approximately how long ago the migration happened.

Skin color is both a biological topic of conversation and a social-political one. But skin color is simply a physical trait. Learn more in this video.

 Biointeractive skin color

By mapping the appearance and frequency of genetic markers in modern humans, scientists are building a picture of where and when our ancient ancestors moved around the globe. Both fossil and DNA evidence support the idea that our species, *Homo sapiens*, originated in Africa around 200,000 years ago. According to both the genetic and paleontological evidence, our human ancestors began to leave Africa between 60,000 and 70,000 years ago. Scientists believe that major cooling in the earth's climate at the time may have driven our ancestors to find new places to live.

Remember, the human genome has about 3 billion bases. While 99.9 percent of our genome is identical, the tiny differences that are passed down from generation to generation can be used to track the movement of populations around the world. By sequencing the DNA of groups of people who have lived in the same area for generations, scientists can analyze and identify the base differences that are common for people in that area.

Using this information, they can determine the likely migration paths that our human ancestors took out of Africa and around the world.

Based on fossil records and the new information provided by genome sequencing, our human ancestors divided into several different groups and moved around the African continent and the world in multiple waves. One of the first waves leaving Africa traveled along the coastline of Asia toward Indonesia. Some traveled thousands of miles until they reached Australia. Evidence to support this idea was found in people living in isolated Indian villages along the route—people who share a rare genetic marker with those who migrated to Australia. Those who still have the genetic marker are probably descendants of the original coastal migrants.

A little later, another group traveled north into the Middle East and southern Central Asia. From these areas, smaller groups broke off and traveled to Europe, northern Asia, and beyond. Later migrations moved our ancestors into Western Europe and Siberia. About 20,000 years ago, ancient humans crossed an ice bridge that connected Asia and present-day Alaska. These migrants and their descendants formed populations in North and South America.

GENETIC DIVERSITY

As humans migrated out of Africa, the genomes of the different groups also began to evolve as they faced new climates, diets, and diseases. Those who carried or developed a genetic mutation that gave them an advantage in their new environment were more likely to survive and produce offspring.

GENE GENIUS

So far, the oldest complete genome comes from a horse discovered in frozen ground in Yukon, Canada. Scientists estimate that the horse fossil is between 560,000 and 780,000 years old.

Check out this interactive map of human migration! Where do your more immediate ancestors come from? Does this make you think about how all humans are related?

 Nat Geo human journey

GENE GENIUS

The PopHumanScan project is producing an extensive catalog of regions in the human genome that show evidence of natural selection. The project uses genome information from the 1000 Genomes Project (1000GP) to locate and identify these genetic adaptations.

GRANDPA!

Did you know that your DNA might reveal a Neanderthal ancestor? As our human ancestors migrated from Africa to different areas around the world, they may have encountered and mated with ancient hominins who also lived tens and hundreds of thousands of years ago. Scientists have found distinct genetic markers from these ancient hominins in the DNA of people living today. This means that you might have a small percentage of your DNA (between 0 to 2 percent) from a Neanderthal ancestor, even though the Neanderthal species has long been extinct. You're living history!

These favorable genetic mutations were passed down from generation to generation.

As time passed, the favorable mutations became common in people living in a specific region. Also, those who lived in the same region were more likely to meet and produce offspring. As a result, two people living near each other were more likely to share the same genetic patterns than two people who lived far apart. This made people living in India more genetically similar to each other than they were to people living in Ireland.

Researchers with the PopHumanScan collaborative catalog project have found genetic evidence of adaptations in more than 2,800 regions of the human genome. Remember, an adaptation is a trait that has evolved through natural selection because it is favorable and gives an organism an advantage. These genetic variations show us how our ancestors were shaped by the different environments and conditions they faced around the world.

One example of a genetic adaptation is the ability to digest lactose, a sugar found in milk. In the human genome, a gene codes for an enzyme that the body uses to digest lactose. In ancient humans, the gene was turned on to produce the enzyme in young children so they could digest their mother's milk. After the child was old enough to be weaned, the gene usually turned off and the lactose-digesting enzyme was no longer produced.

However, around 5,000 years ago, a genetic adaptation occurred in the cattle-herding people of northern Europe. This population relied on cattle and cattle milk for many nutrients.

People who had a gene mutation that allowed them to digest lactose as adults had a survival advantage because it was easier for them to consume more nutrients. The genetic adaptation that kept the lactose gene turned on into adulthood spread throughout the population.

Genomic studies have found that this genetic adaptation for lactose tolerance was not limited to the northern Europeans. Researchers have tested multiple ethnic groups in East Africa and discovered three separate mutations, all of which were different from the one found in the Europeans, all of which kept the lactose gene turned on in adults.

Lactose tolerance had evolved independently at least four times in the human genome—an example of convergent evolution. Natural selection allowed people with the different mutations to pass on that mutation to future generations. In Africa, people with the lactose gene mutation produced 10 times more offspring, which gave them a strong advantage in spreading the mutation across the population.

Researchers studying other genes have also found adaptation evidence for genes that control skin color, salt retention, resistance to malaria, and more. And the change has not stopped. The story of human evolution is still being written. As scientists learn more about the human genome, they hope to unlock more chapters in the human story. Who knows what the future might bring? We'll study at least a few answers to that question next!

VOCAB LAB

Write down what you think each word means. What root words can you find to help you? What does the context of the word tell you?

ancestor, **descendant**, **environment**, **evolution**, **fossil**, **migration**, and **species**

Compare your definitions with those of your friends or classmates. Did you all come up with the same meanings? Turn to the text and glossary if you need help.

TEXT TO WORLD

Do you know where your ancestors came from? Do some research to learn how your family arrived at the place you live today.

KEY QUESTIONS

- **Why might it be important to know what region of the world someone's ancestors lived when considering their health and well-being?**

NATURAL SELECTION

Natural selection is the process by which some organisms with certain traits that help them better adapt to their environment tend to survive and produce more offspring. In this activity, you will demonstrate how natural selection works.

Ideas for Supplies

- three types of beans, each in a different color, 50 beans per type
- two different colored backgrounds, such as colored paper

- **To start, spread all of the beans onto one colored background.** Close your eyes for about 30 seconds. Open them and pick up the first bean your eye is drawn to. Close your eyes again for 10 seconds and repeat. Repeat 20 times.

- **Count the remaining beans on the background.** Count the beans removed.

- **Create a chart that shows how many of each bean you removed.**

- **Repeat all steps using the second colored background.** Create a data chart for your results.

- **Based on your results, think about the following questions.**

  - On background #1, which bean survived the best? Which bean was the worst survivor? Why do you think this happened? Predict what will happen to this population of beans over time. Explain your prediction.

  - On background #2, which bean survived the best? Which bean survived the worst? Was this a different result from background #1? Why?

  - Why do different beans survive better on different backgrounds?

  - How does this activity simulate natural selection? How does natural selection help explain the story of human evolution?

To investigate more, is there a background/ environment in which none of the beans would have an advantage? Why? What might happen to this population?

Chapter 6 ▶
Our Genomic Future

How might genomics help us in the future?

UNDERSTANDING THE GENOME IS REALLY CHANGING OUR LIVES.

I'M REALLY EXCITED ABOUT THE WAYS IT'S GOING TO CHANGE OUR FUTURE!

ME, TOO! IMAGINE ALL THE DIFFERENT FIELDS THAT IT'S GOING TO AFFECT!

HISTORY AND ARCHAEOLOGY!

AGRICULTURE!

FORENSICS!

MEDICINE!

THOSE ARE GREAT, BUT I'M *REALLY* HOPING THEY INVENT ICE CREAM-FLAVORED KALE SOMETIME SOON.

MY DAD COOKS *SO* MUCH KALE.

WITH GENOMICS, EVEN THAT DREAM COULD COME TRUE.

By understanding the human genome better and improving on ways of manipulating the genome, we might be able to improve the health and well-being of all people. But some experts are concerned that we could do more damage than good.

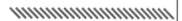

We've looked at the past, the distant past, and the future to see how mapping the human genome contributes to our understanding of the human species (and other species) and how we can use that understanding to improve lives. Scientists continue to work every day to learn more about the human genome and how it impacts medicine, evolutionary biology, and other areas. Research studies that build on the work of the Human Genome Project are in progress around the world.

As their work unlocks new secrets in the human genome, genomics has the potential to profoundly alter our lives in many ways. What might the future look like as we learn more about our genes and how to manipulate them?

At the same time, how this genomic information is used and who has access to it is becoming an increasing concern.

DELICIOUS GENOMICS?

Genomics has increased our understanding of many different organisms. More than 5,000 organisms have had their genomes sequenced or are in the process of being done. Many more will be at least partially sequenced. The information we gain from sequencing other species' genomes is important to humans in many ways.

For example, genomics is helping farmers improve our food supply. In the past, farmers selectively bred plants with desirable qualities, such as pest resistance or increased seed production.

The corn on the cob we know today is a result of thousands of years of artificial selection.

Across generations of selective breeding, most of the farmer's plants carried the desirable traits. However, the process was extremely time consuming—it took years! Now, the ability to read genome sequences along with new technologies that allow scientists to add new genes or change genes already in a plant's genome enable farmers to speed up the process of selective breeding.

Scientists can selectively add genes that code for favorable traits into crops. The resulting crops are called genetically modified organisms (GMOs).

Golden rice is one example of a GMO crop. This type of rice has tiny pieces of corn and bacterial DNA added to its genome. These added genes make the rice produce beta carotene, which helps the human body maintain healthy skin and mucus membranes, healthy immune systems, and eye health and vision. Scientists see golden rice as a tool to fight vitamin A deficiency worldwide and improve lives.

Do you eat GMOs? Watch this video and find out!

Smithsonian GMO video

A company called Kraig has genetically engineered a new kind of silk fiber that is very strong and flexible.

Genome sequencing is also being used in cattle and other animals to speed up and improve selective breeding, just like what's being done for plants. In Brazil, scientists are using genomics to find specific genome sequences in bulls, allowing them to select for the genes that will produce animals that grow faster and thrive on grass feeding to avoid the need to supplement the bulls' food with grain. This is both cheaper and faster for farmers.

As the world's population grows, the need for secure food supplies to fight world hunger will also rise. To meet the world's food demands, farmers can use genomics and genomic technologies to improve their crops and livestock.

FOOD FOR THOUGHT

Some people think we should be careful with genetically modified food, since there is little known about the long-term effects on human health. In fact, people have experienced unwanted side effects when eating GM foods, such as allergic reactions. Plus, GM food might have reduced nutritional value. GM crops can also have a negative effect on the environment, releasing toxins and disrupting biodiversity.

NABBING CRIMINALS

It was not long ago when blood at a crime scene was the best evidence a detective could find. Crime labs ran tests on the blood to determine its type and used this information to narrow down a list of suspects. However, matching a blood type to a suspect was not conclusive proof that they committed a crime. Even the rarest blood type is shared by about 2 million people in the United States—that's a lot of suspects!

Now, genomics is leading to new and better forensic crime scene analysis.

People leave behind traces of their DNA all the time, through skin cells, hairs, or other body fluids. At a crime scene, investigators collect these traces and send them to forensic labs for analysis. In the lab, scientists can use powerful technologies to amplify and sequence even the tiniest amounts of DNA. They compare the crime scene sample to samples from known suspects.

If they do not have a known suspect, they can upload the crime scene sample sequence into large DNA databases, such as the Combined DNA Index System (CODIS), which store DNA profiles from millions of people collected by federal, state, and local laboratories.

CODIS's computer software searches through its database to find a match to the sample. It compares 20 areas of DNA across the human genome. When it finds a DNA match, investigators can identify the criminal.

DO-IT-YOURSELF GENOME TESTING

Want to learn more about your own genome? Did you know that you could buy an at-home test that will give you information about your genome? Since the Human Genome Project, advances in genomics have led to a number of companies providing personal genomic testing.

This form of at-home testing, called direct-to-consumer genomic testing, allows a person to get genomic information without involving a doctor. People can purchase testing kits and collect DNA samples from saliva, mail them to the lab, and receive the results of their genome—all from the privacy of their own homes.

GENE GENIUS

Forensic scientists are using DNA analyses to identify remains from the September 11, 2001, terror attacks at the World Trade Center site in New York City and to identify remains of soldiers from the Vietnam War.

Some family trees are pretty complex!

credit: Herry Lawford (CC BY 2.0)

One popular reason people use at-home genomic tests is to learn more about their family ancestry. The company Ancestry.com started as a website where people could search historical and family records to learn more about their family history.

The company has expanded its services to offer genomic tests for people who want to learn more about their genomic ancestry. Since it started offering the tests, millions of customers have jumped at the chance to discover more about their genome.

Other genomic testing companies, such as 23andMe.com (founded in 2006), offer genomic testing for people interested in learning health, traits, and ancestry information. These tests can tell you if you have dry or wet earwax because of a genomic variation or if your genes cause you to prefer salty and savory treats over sweet snacks.

These tests can also tell if you have a genetic predisposition to many common conditions, such as Alzheimer's disease, celiac disease, and Parkinson's disease.

23andMe.com also gives customers the chance to provide their genomic information to large research studies. This helps to advance genomic science and improve human health.

Could this system have a downside? There has been some debate about the pros and cons of at-home genomic testing. Some people believe that the more information they have about their health, ancestry, and family connections the better off they are. However, users should be careful to determine if the particular company they've chosen is reputable and if the science behind the test is validated. Users should also ask if the specific test they want to take has been approved by the U.S. Food and Drug Administration.

> Plus, a genome test reveals only one part of a person's complete health picture.

Other factors, including environment and lifestyle, contribute to a person's risk of disease. Taking an at-home test should not be a replacement for talking with a qualified genetic counselor or health care provider to determine what steps, if any, a person should take to protect their health.

The hope for almost every scientific breakthrough is to improve lives. Watch this video about a genomic medical success story.

 NIH Zarko story

EPIGENETICS: THROWING THE SWITCH

As scientists locate more genes on the human genome, they also study how and why certain genes are expressed and how environmental factors affect this process. Remember, gene expression is when a gene is turned on and its information becomes active or useful—for example, a gene that is actively creating a particular protein.

Take a look at this video to learn more about epigenetics and how the environment can affect us on a genetic level!

 Vimeo UW EDGE epigenetics

Throughout a person's lifetime, genes get turned on or off, like switches. Epigenetics is the study of changes in DNA regulation that are caused by the environment and get passed down to offspring.

Scientists have discovered that certain chemical compounds can change gene activity on a single gene. The chemical compounds are not part of the DNA sequence, but are attached to the DNA, like a backpack is attached to a student but is not part of their body. These attached compounds remain even as the cells divide. In some cases, the changes are even passed down to future generations—but still, they do not change the underlying DNA sequence. These changes are known as epigenetic.

> Epigenetic changes affect which genes are turned on and off. They can influence whether a cell produces proteins or not.

In many cases, epigenetic changes are a normal part of cell operations—they make sure the right cells produce the right proteins. For example, epigenetic modifications ensure that proteins that promote bone growth are produced by bone cells and not by muscle cells.

Sometimes, errors occur in the epigenetic process. Certain factors in the environment, such as diet or pollution, can interrupt epigenetic changes. In some cases, this alters how a gene performs. The gene may stop working completely or it may stay turned on for too long.

Although some errors have little impact on an organism, others can cause a lot of damage. Some epigenetic errors have been linked to genetic disorders and conditions, including cancers, metabolic disorders, and degenerative diseases.

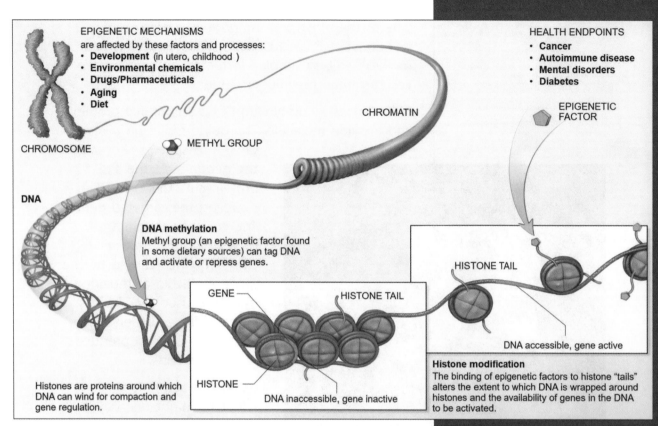

EPIGENETIC MECHANISMS
are affected by these factors and processes:
- **Development** (in utero, childhood)
- **Environmental chemicals**
- **Drugs/Pharmaceuticals**
- **Aging**
- **Diet**

HEALTH ENDPOINTS
- **Cancer**
- **Autoimmune disease**
- **Mental disorders**
- **Diabetes**

CHROMOSOME

CHROMATIN

METHYL GROUP

EPIGENETIC FACTOR

DNA

DNA methylation
Methyl group (an epigenetic factor found in some dietary sources) can tag DNA and activate or repress genes.

HISTONE TAIL

GENE

HISTONE TAIL

DNA accessible, gene active

HISTONE

DNA inaccessible, gene inactive

Histones are proteins around which DNA can wind for compaction and gene regulation.

Histone modification
The binding of epigenetic factors to histone "tails" alters the extent to which DNA is wrapped around histones and the availability of genes in the DNA to be activated.

Epigenetic mechanisms infographic from the National Institutes of Health

Scientists are trying to understand genes and the chemical compounds that modify them. They hope that by learning how epigenetic changes control gene function and protein production, they will be able to develop new treatments for genetic disease caused by these errors.

USING THE ERASER—ON GENES!

What if it were possible to change your DNA? One of the most exciting areas for future genetic research involves genome editing, which allows scientists to make precise, targeted changes to the genes of living cells. Genome editing could allow them to treat disease by replacing defective genes.

One of the most promising gene-editing technologies is called CRISPR. CRISPR has made genome editing simpler, faster, cheaper, and more accurate than previous methods.

CRISPR uses a combination of a scissor-like protein and a guide molecule. The guide molecule takes CRISPR to specific sites within the genome. At the site, the protein cuts the cell's DNA, disabling the targeted gene. The cell then repairs the DNA by putting in a new DNA sequence carried by the guide molecule or repairing the cut caused by CRISPR's scissors. The cell then uses the edited DNA to produce healthy proteins.

Using this technology, scientists might one day be able to delete undesirable traits from the genome and add desirable ones, without hurting anything else in the body.

Maybe CRISPR could be used to edit a gene that causes diabetes and other chronic diseases.

In 2017, scientists reported a breakthrough. They used CRISPR technology to edit a dangerous mutation from a human embryo, correct it, and create a healthy embryo.

This development illustrated that genome editing may one day be able to protect babies from a variety of genetic conditions—even before they are born. Because their DNA was repaired, the embryos would not pass the mutation along to descendants.

Scientists caution that more research is needed before the gene-editing method can even be tested in clinical trials.

Yet in the future, such a technique may be able to help families have healthy children. It could potentially be used to correct the more than 10,000 conditions caused by inherited gene mutations, including breast and ovarian cancer linked to gene mutations, along with diseases such as Huntington's, Tay-Sachs, cystic fibrosis, and early-onset Alzheimer's.

Although genome editing with CRISPR is a promising technology for treating disease, it is not without risks. In some cases, CRISPR can edit the wrong place in a genome. When this occurs, it could introduce mutations at the wrong point rather than the targeted location.

Even when genome editing modifies a genome precisely as intended, the change might not always have the expected outcome. For example, in some HIV studies using CRISPR, the HIV virus developed new mutations that allowed it to survive the CRISPR edits and start replicating again.

In order to use genome editing effectively to treat disease, scientists will need to develop a precise delivery system that works to deliver a gene addition to a specific body location. Scientists will need to make sure that the human body does not view the CRISPR tool or the delivery components as invaders, triggering the body's immune system to attack.

GENE GENIUS

Groups such as The Innocence Project are using DNA analyses to exonerate people years after being accused or convicted of a crime by showing their DNA does not match the sample collected at the crime scene.

In addition to the practical concerns of what could go wrong when using CRISPR, what about the moral concerns? While curing disease is an honorable use of technology, what if we get to the point where we can decide what other traits a person will have? Should parents be able to decide their baby's future self?

All of these questions should be considered as we learn more about genome editing.

"I Think They Were Tall . . ."

When trying to track and identify a suspect, a police sketch artist will often sit down with any eyewitnesses and draw a picture of the suspect based on their descriptions. Now, scientists are working to develop a way to create a police sketch based on DNA collected at a crime scene. While a person's DNA cannot yet predict their facial appearance, it can be used to identify some traits, such as hair color and eye color, that may be useful for investigators. One day, forensic scientists may be able to determine even more about a suspect's physical appearance simply from the DNA they left at the crime scene.

EVEN IF WE CAN . . . SHOULD WE?

As science explores new frontiers of the human genome, many ethical and social concerns have been brought up. Who should have access to genomic information? How should it be used? Just because genomic testing and editing is possible, should it be done?

These questions are just some of the complicated issues that emerge as we unlock more and more of the human genome.

In 1990, the scientists who launched the Human Genome Project recognized that having a complete human genome sequence would raise many concerns. They established the Ethical, Legal, and Social Implications (ELSI) Research Program at the NIH as part of the Human Genome Project. The ELSI program supports research aimed at understanding how genomic research impacts individuals, families, and communities.

Questions about consent and privacy are one area of study in ELSI research. What does a person need to know about a research study before they agree to donate their DNA?

It's a concept called informed consent, which means that the participant understands the purpose and risks of the research before deciding to participate. As new areas of genomic study have emerged, researchers have needed to update their guidelines to help people understand the risks and benefits of being a research participant.

Privacy is another concern for genomic data. When a test is performed on a person's DNA, how does the research or medical facility keep the person's genomic data confidential? Does that meet the person's privacy needs?

Since each person shares part of their genome with parents and children, should a person be able to stop a relative from revealing genomic information with others?

GENETIC INFORMATION NONDISCRIMINATION ACT

Could genomic information be used to discriminate against people in the future? What if a potential employer decides not to hire a job applicant because they have a high risk of developing cancer? What if a health insurance company denies coverage because a person has a genomic mutation that makes them likely to develop bipolar disorder? In 2008, U.S. President George W. Bush (1946–) signed the Genetic Information Nondiscrimination Act into law. The law specifically protects job applicants and current employees from discrimination because of their genetic information. The law also bans health insurers from discriminating against anyone based on their genome.

Watch this video to learn more about how CRISPR works.

 STAT CRISPR works

Another privacy concern is whether or not a person should be given back all of their data from a genomic research study or clinical test. When genomic testing is involved, this can be a lot of data. Most research studies do not return data to participants, while clinical or at-home genomic testing might give participants more data. Participants may want to share their personal genomic data with other groups or health care professionals.

> There are also privacy concerns about what the organizations do with genomic data. How would you feel if your genetic information was part of a study used to develop a new kind of weapon?

The human genome holds the instructions for everything our body's cells do throughout our lifetime. By studying the human genome, scientists have learned fundamental details about life and have answered basic questions about heredity, how cells work, and how living things have evolved. A growing understanding of genomics has given scientists tools to treat and better understand disease and to develop life-changing technologies in areas from agriculture to forensic science to genome editing.

As science unlocks more secrets in the human genome, the possibilities are endless.

TEXT TO WORLD

Have you or any family members done a direct-to-consumer genetics test? Did the results surprise you?

KEY QUESTIONS

- What are some ways a person's individual rights might be overlooked with home genetics tests?
- What are some of the dangers of gene editing? Do the benefits outweigh the potential drawbacks?

GENOME TESTING FOR THE ATHLETE

Some direct-to-consumer genomic testing companies claim to be able to provide a wide variety of information about a person, including whether or not they have the potential to be a successful athlete. These tests track genetic markers that are associated with speed and power or endurance. Imagine that your school decides to conduct genomic testing on high school athletes to determine which sports they should play. Should these tests be used? Why or why not? Should the results be public to anyone?

- **What are the positive effects of this genome testing?** How does this testing and the information it provides improve the lives of athletes and students in the school?

- **What are the negative effects of genome testing?** What risks arise from this testing and the information it provides?

- **Do you think people should use genomic testing to identify people with certain skills and talents?** Does your answer change based on the age of the person being tested? Does it change based on the trait being tested?

- **Write a brief essay that explains your point of view on genomic testing for skills and talents.** Be sure to include an introductory paragraph, separate paragraphs for each of your three main points, and a conclusion. Share your essay with your class.

VOCAB LAB 📖

Write down what you think each word means. What root words can you find to help you? What does the context of the word tell you?

CRISPR, epigenetics, ethical, forensic, genetically modified organism, genome editing, informed consent, and **selective breeding**.

Compare your definitions with those of your friends or classmates. Did you all come up with the same meanings? Turn to the text and glossary if you need help.

To investigate more, write a persuasive essay taking the other side. Use your essay to convince the reader to agree with your position.

CUT WITH MOLECULAR SCISSORS

To edit a genome, scientists use a restriction enzyme to cut a piece of DNA. A restriction enzyme is a protein that acts like a pair of scissors and cuts a DNA strand. The enzyme (called a cutter) recognizes a specific DNA sequence where it will cut.

Once cut, the DNA can be put back together in different ways. Sometimes, a new gene is inserted. Other times, a diseased gene is removed. Cutting DNA with molecular scissors is a very important part of genome editing. Yet, how do restriction enzymes know where to cut a DNA strand? In this activity, you will use a computer program to test a DNA sequence and identify restriction enzymes that will cut it.

- **To start, create a DNA sequence (using the A, T, C, and G bases).** Your DNA sequence should be 20 bases long.

- **Next, enter your DNA sequence into the NEBcutter program from New England Biolabs.** Submit the sequence. NEBcutter sequence

- **The program will return a page with the DNA sequence and one or more enzymes that cut it.** This is a restriction enzyme map. Each arrow on the map shows where a restriction enzyme will cut the DNA strand. It also shows the name of the enzyme that will cut in that location. How many restriction enzymes cut the DNA strand?

- **Now, change your DNA sequence and enter the new sequence into the NEBcutter program.** What restriction enzymes cut the new sequence? Did changing the sequence change the restriction enzymes that cut it?

- **Repeat this analysis with at least five different DNA sequences.** Each time you will use a new DNA sequence and make a restriction enzyme map.

- **Compare all of the DNA sequences and restriction enzyme maps.**

  - Is there an enzyme that appears in more than one map?

  - Is there an enzyme that appears in all of the maps?

  - Do any of the restriction enzymes appear on only one map?

  - Does changing the DNA sequence change the restriction enzymes needed to cut the DNA?

  - What does this tell you about the relationship between DNA sequences and restriction enzymes?

- **Create a table to summarize and display your data.**

To investigate more, consider whether the length of a DNA sequence changes the number of restriction enzymes used to cut it. Take one of the DNA sequences used above and increase it to 40 bases, 60 bases, and 100 bases. Run each through the NEBcutter program. Which sequence has the most cutters? Do longer sequences have more cutters than short sequences?

Inquire & Investigate ▶

TO CATCH A THIEF

DNA collected from a crime scene can link a suspect to the evidence, placing a person at a crime scene, even if they claim not to have been there. When investigators have a suspect, they often obtain a DNA sample and compare it to the DNA evidence at the scene. In this activity, you will use DNA profiling to figure out which suspect robbed a jewelry store.

- **You've been called in to examine DNA evidence from a jewelry store heist.** The police recovered a hair at the crime scene that belongs to the thief. When comparing a DNA sample to profiles in its CODIS database, the FBI looks at 13 loci in the human genome, areas that are likely to have differences unique to an individual. For this activity, you'll use three loci to narrow down a list of three suspects. Note that each DNA sample in the charts below has nucleotides from two chromosomes (one from the individual's mother, one from their father). Both chromosomes must match to show the hair at the crime scene came from a suspect.

LOCUS 1							
Hair evidence		Suspect 1		Suspect 2		Suspect 3	
G	G	A	G	A	G	T	G
T	T	C	C	C	C	C	G
A	A	A	G	G	G	A	G
G		C	G	T	T	G	G
T		G	G	A	A	T	A
A		T	T	G	T	A	A
G		A	A	T	A	G	T
T		G	G	A	G	T	G
A		A	T	G	T	A	A
		A	A	T	C	A	A
		T	G	A	G	T	T
		G	T	G	T	G	C
		A	A	A	A	A	T

Answers: 1) Suspect 1 and Suspect 2, 2) Suspect 2, 3) Suspect 2, 4) Based on the DNA evidence, suspect 2

LOCUS 2							
Hair evidence		Suspect 1		Suspect 2		Suspect 3	
T	T	T	G	A	G	T	T
T	T	T	C	C	C	T	T
T	T	C	T	G	G	T	T
C	C	G	C	T	T	C	C
	T	G	G	A	A	T	A
	T	T	T	T	T	A	T
	T	T	C	T	T	G	T
	C	T	C	T	T	T	T
		T	T	C	C	A	C
		C	A	T	T	A	A
		G	G	A	T	T	T
		G	T	G	T	G	C
		A	A	A	C	A	T

LOCUS 3							
Hair evidence		Suspect 1		Suspect 2		Suspect 3	
C	C	A	G	C	C	C	C
G	G	C	C	G	G	G	G
C	C	A	G	C	C	C	C
G	G	C	G	G	G	G	G
C	C	G	G	C	C	T	A
G	G	T	T	G	G	A	A
C	C	C	C	C	C	G	T
G	G	G	G	G	G	T	G
C	C	C	C	C	C	A	A
G	G	G	G	G	G	A	A
		T	G	A	G	T	T
		G	T	G	T	G	C
		A	A	A	A	A	T

1. Which suspect's DNA matches the DNA of the evidence hair at locus site 1?

2. Which suspect's DNA matches the DNA of the evidence hair at locus site 2?

3. Which suspect's DNA matches the DNA of the evidence hair at locus site 3?

4. Which suspect do you believe is the jewelry thief?

5. How certain are you of your results? What could you do to increase your certainty?

To investigate more, consider in what scenarios DNA profiling would give investigators an incorrect answer. How could this happen? What can investigators and forensic analysts do to prevent errors in crime scene DNA analysis?

GLOSSARY

abnormality: a difference from what is normal, usually in a negative way.

actin: a protein that combines to form the thin filament of the muscle fiber.

adapt: to make a change to survive in new or different conditions.

adaptation: random mutations in DNA that enable animals to survive longer.

allele: one of the forms of a gene found at a particular point on a chromosome.

ambassador: someone who represents their country or an item that represents a region.

amino acid: a molecule made of hydrogen, oxygen, carbon, and nitrogen atoms that links with other amino acids to form a protein chain.

amplify: to make many copies.

ancestor: someone from your family who lived before you.

ancient DNA: DNA extracted from ancient remains.

antibodies: proteins that help the immune system fight infections or bacteria.

archaeology: the study of ancient people through the objects they left behind.

artifact: an object made by a human being in an earlier time.

assembler: a program for converting data into more useable information.

atom: a very small piece of matter. Atoms are the tiny building blocks that make up everything in the universe.

authenticate: to prove that something is real or genuine.

autoimmune disease: a disease that causes the body to attack healthy cells.

autosomal chromosome: any chromosome except for the sex chromosomes.

bacteria: microorganisms found in soil, water, plants, and animals. Some are harmful, while others are helpful. Singular is bacterium.

behavioral: having to do with the way an organism acts and interacts with its environment and other organisms in order to survive.

biodiversity: the range of living things in an area.

bioinformatics: a field of science that combines biology, computer science, engineering, mathematics, and statistics to analyze and interpret biological data.

biological function: what an organ, tissue, cell, or molecule does.

biological parent: a child's natural parent, either the male who supplied the sperm or the female who supplied the egg.

biology: the study of life and living things.

blueprint: a model or template to follow.

carbon: an element found in all organic compounds.

cardiovascular system: the body system that includes the heart and blood vessels. Also called the circulatory system.

cell: the smallest unit of life.

cell membrane: the cell's thin outer boundary.

centromere: a region of a chromosome that appears during cell division where sister chromatids are held together.

characteristic: a feature of a person, such as blue eyes or curly hair.

chemical: a substance that has certain features that can react with other substances.

chemotherapy: drugs used to treat cancer.

chromatin: a mass of genetic material made of DNA and proteins that condense to form chromosomes during eukaryotic cell division.

chromosome: the part of a cell that contains genes.

circulating tumor DNA (ct DNA): small pieces of DNA from cancerous cells and tumors that are found in the bloodstream.

climate: the average weather patterns in an area during a long period of time.

clone-by-clone sequencing: a method of DNA sequencing in which a map of each chromosome in the genome is made before the DNA is split into fragments for sequencing.

clone: a genetic copy.

codon: a combination of three nucleotides in mRNA that translates to an amino acid.

collaboration: to work together, a group effort.

comparative genomics: a field of science that compares the genomes of different species.

compile: to gather.

complementary: forces or people that work together.

composite: combining two or more to make a single picture.

compound: a substance made up of two or more elements. The elements are held together by bonds just as molecules are held together by bonds. Compounds are not easily separated. Water is a compound.

consensus: a general agreement.

contaminate: to make impure or dirty by contact or mixture with another substance.

convergent evolution: the process by which organisms independently evolve similar traits because of adapting to similar environments.

CRISPR: a type of genome-editing technology that allows scientists to cut DNA at a targeted location.

crops: plants grown for food and other uses.

cytoplasm: the jelly-like fluid inside a cell.

data set: a collection of data.

decode: translate a coded message.

decompose: to break down into simpler elements.

deletion: a mutation in which all or part of a chromosome is missing.

denature: to separate.

deoxyribose: a sugar used to make DNA.

descendant: a person related to someone who lived in the past.

diagnose: to identify an illness or condition.

diagnostic testing: a medical procedure performed to gather information to make a decision or diagnosis.

digestion: the process of breaking down food that is eaten.

digestive system: the body system responsible for receiving and digesting food, absorbing nutrients, and eliminating what is not needed.

discriminate: to unfairly treat a person or group differently from others, usually because of their race, gender, or age.

DNA (deoxyribonucleic acid): a chemical that carries genetic instruction for how the body should grow and function.

DNA fingerprint: a description of the pattern of genes in an organism's DNA.

DNA sequencing: to determine the order of nucleotide bases in a strand of DNA.

dominant: a genetic trait that hides the expression of a recessive trait.

electrode: a conductor through which electricity enters or leaves an object, substance, or region.

element: a pure substance that cannot be broken down into a simpler substance. Everything in the universe is made up of combinations of elements. Oxygen, gold, and carbon are three elements.

embryo: the earliest stage of development for a living animal.

endangered: a species of plant or animal that is at risk of disappearing entirely.

environment: everything in nature, living and nonliving, including animals, plants, rocks, soil, and water.

environmental: relating to the natural world, the impact of human activity on its condition, and its impact on humans.

enzyme: a chemical in living things that speeds up or slows down reactions.

epidemic: a disease that hits large groups at the same time and spreads quickly.

epigenetics: the study of changes in organisms caused by changes in gene expression, not in changes of the DNA itself.

ethical: acting in a way that upholds someone's belief in right and wrong.

eukaryotic cell: a cell that has a nucleus enclosed within membranes, unlike prokaryotes, which have no membrane-bound organelles.

evolution: the process of living things gradually changing to adapt to the world around them.

GLOSSARY

evolutionary biology: the branch of biology that studies the origin of life and the diversification and adaptation of life forms over time.

exon: a part of a gene that contains coding DNA.

exonerate: to absolve from blame for a fault or wrongdoing.

extract: to remove or take out by effort or force.

fertilize: to join female and male cells to produce seeds and offspring.

forensic: applying scientific methods to the investigation of a crime.

fossils: the preserved remains of a dead organisms or the remains of an organism's actions.

fragment: a small piece.

gel electrophoresis: a laboratory method used to separate mixtures of DNA according to molecular size.

gender: male or female, and their roles or behavior defined by society.

gene: a section of DNA that codes for a particular trait.

gene annotation: the process of locating genes and the coding regions in a genome and identifying what those areas do.

gene expression: when a gene is turned on and its information becomes active or useful.

gene prediction: the process of identifying the regions of genomic DNA that encode genes.

gene regulation: the mechanisms that cells use to turn a gene on or off.

genetic: relating to genes, which are units of DNA and RNA that assign organisms their characteristics.

genetics: the study of genes and heredity.

genetic code: the sequence of nucleotides in DNA or RNA that determines the specific amino acid sequence when building proteins.

genetic disease: a disease or condition that results from an inability of a gene or genes to function normally.

genetic marker: a gene or short sequence of DNA used to identify a chromosome or to locate other genes on a genetic map.

genetic variation: a different form of a gene.

genetically modified organism (GMO): an organism whose DNA has been altered using genetic engineering.

geneticist: a scientist who studies inheritance.

genome: an organism's complete set of DNA.

genome editing: the process of making changes to an organism's genome.

genome map: a map of all the genes in an organism.

genome-wide association study: a study that compares the entire genomes of many organisms to identify genetic variation.

genomic medicine: using a person's genome to make better health care decisions.

genomics: the analysis of complete genomic sequences from different organisms.

glucose: a basic sugar that provides energy.

haplotype: a group of genes in an organism that is inherited from a single parent.

helix: spiral in form.

heredity: the passing of characteristics from one generation to the next.

histone: a protein that helps DNA coil into compact units.

hominin: a group of primates that includes recent humans together with extinct ancestral and related forms.

hormone: a chemical that travels through the bloodstream to signal other cells to do their job in the body.

Human Genome Project (HGP): an effort by scientists worldwide to identify and map all of the human genome's 3 billion base pairs.

inflammation: when part of the body becomes reddened, swollen, hot, and often painful, especially as a reaction to injury or infection.

informed consent: when a participant understands the risks and benefits of participating in a research study.

inheritance: passing characteristics from parents to offspring.

insulin: a hormone in the body that regulates sugar in the blood.

intron: a segment of DNA that does not code for proteins.

karyotype: a picture of an organism's chromosomes, lined up by size and shape.

lactose: a sugar present in milk.

liquid biopsy: a blood test performed to look for cancer cells from a tumor or pieces of DNA from tumor cells that are in the blood.

livestock: animals raised for food and other uses.

macromolecule: a large molecule, usually made of at least 100 atoms.

manipulate: to handle, use, or control an object in a skillful way.

messenger RNA (mRNA): the form of RNA that transcribes DNA's sequence of bases and transfers that information to a ribosome in the cell.

microbe: a microorganism such as a bacterium.

migrant: an organism that moves from one location to another.

migration: the process of moving from one location to another.

mitochondria: a large organelle with a small amount of DNA that produces energy needed for cellular activities.

mitosis: cell division in which two identical daughter cells are created

model: something used to study the development and progression of disease.

molecular: having to do with molecules, the groups of atoms bound together to form everything.

molecular biology: the branch of biology that deals with the structure and function of the proteins and nucleic acids essential to life.

molecule: a group of atoms, which are the smallest particles of an element, bound together.

moral: the discussion between what is right and what is wrong for a particular issue.

multicellular: an organism with two or more cells.

musculoskeletal: relating to the muscles and bones together.

mutagen: an agent that causes a change in the structure of a gene.

mutation: a permanent change in the DNA of an organism.

myosin: the protein in the thick filament of a muscle fiber.

natural selection: one of the basic means of evolution in which organisms that are well-adapted to their environment are better able to survive, reproduce, and pass along their useful traits to offspring.

Neanderthal: an extinct species from the Homo genus.

nervous system: the communication system of the body, made of nerve cells that connect the brain and extend through the body.

neuron: a single nerve cell that carries messages between the brain and other parts of the body.

nitrogen: an element that is the most common gas in the earth's atmosphere.

noncoding: a section of DNA that does not code for a protein.

nuclear membrane: the membrane that encloses a cell's nucleus.

nucleosome: the repeating subunits of chromatin, consisting of a DNA chain coiled around a core of histones.

nucleotide: a molecule made up of a nitrogen base, sugar, and phosphate group.

nucleus: the part of a cell that controls how it functions. Plural is nuclei.

nutrient: a substance an organism needs to live and grow.

offspring: a child.

organ: a part of the body with a special function, such as the heart, lungs, brain, and skin.

organelle: a structure within a cell that has a special function.

organic: something that is or was living.

organism: any living thing, such as a plant or animal.

GLOSSARY

paleogenetics: the study of the past through the examination of preserved genetic material from the remains of ancient organisms.

pancreas: a gland located in the abdomen that produces enzymes for digestion and for regulating blood sugar.

parasite: a living thing that feeds off another living thing.

patent: a document given to the inventor of something that protects them from someone copying their invention.

personalized: tailoring something for a specific individual.

pharmacogenomics: the study of how genes affect a person's response to a drug.

philanthropic: showing concern for others through charitable actions or donations of funds.

phosphate: an inorganic compound containing the element phosphorous.

point mutation: a mutation caused by a change in a single base on the DNA chain.

polygenic disorder: a disease caused by multiple genes.

polymerase chain reaction (PCR): a process used to make many copies of DNA.

population: organisms in the same group or species that live in the same geographical area.

predator: an animal or plant that kills and eats another animal.

predisposition: a tendency to have a particular condition.

progeria: a rare, genetic disorder that causes premature aging.

protein: a group of large molecules composed of chains of amino acids. Proteins are an essential part of all living things.

public domain: creative materials that are not protected by intellectual property laws such as copyright, trademark, or patent laws.

Punnett square: a diagram that is used to predict an outcome of a genetic cross or breeding experiment.

radiation: a form of electromagnetic energy that can cause harm to humans and other living creatures, as well as a form of treatment for diseases such as cancer.

radioactive: having or producing a powerful form of energy known as radioactivity.

recessive: a trait that is not expressed when a dominant trait is present.

red blood cells: blood cells that contain hemoglobin, which allows them to carry oxygen and carbon dioxide through the bloodstream.

reference genome: a genome that has already been sequenced that can be used for comparison.

regulatory: intended to control something.

relapse: a reoccurrence of a previous medical condition.

remission: having no signs of disease, particularly cancer.

replicate: to make a copy.

reproductive system: a system of organs that work together for the purpose of sexual reproduction.

reputable: generally considered to be honest and reliable.

respiration: the act of breathing, a process in living organisms that involves the production of energy, typically with the intake of oxygen and the release of carbon dioxide in animals or the intake of carbon dioxide and the release of oxygen in plants.

retention: the continued possession of something.

ribosomal RNA (rRNA): a noncoding type of RNA that acts as the primary building block for ribosomes and the assembly line where protein building occurs in ribosomes.

ribosome: an organelle found in cells that translates messenger RNA into protein.

schizophrenia: a brain disorder in which people interpret reality abnormally.

scientific inquiry: an approach to teaching and learning science based on questions, experiments, and evaluation of data.

screening: checking for disease even when there are no symptoms.

selective breeding: a process used by humans to develop new organisms with desirable characteristics.

sequence: the order in which something happens or to determine the order in which something happens.

sex chromosome: one of a pair of chromosomes that determines if an organism is male or female.

single nucleotide polymorphism (SNP): a variation in a single base pair in a DNA sequence.

single-gene disease: any genetic disorder caused by a change affecting only one gene.

social: relating to people's lives in a group and to rules about behavior with other people.

species: a group of plants or animals that are closely related and produce offspring.

spherical: shaped round, like a ball.

splice: to connect the ends of two things so that they form one piece.

statistics: the practice or science of collecting and analyzing numerical data in large quantities.

stimulus: a change in an organism's environment that causes an action, activity, or response. Plural is stimuli.

subclone: a variation in a cancer's genome.

survival advantage: any factor in an organism's environment, health, or physical development that gives it an advantage that makes it more likely to survive.

susceptible: likely to be influenced or harmed by something.

synthesize: to build.

taq polymerase: an enzyme used in PCR technology to build new strands of DNA.

technology: the tools, methods, and systems used to solve a problem or do work.

telomere: the tip of a chromosome.

template: a pattern or model to build a copy of something.

thermocycler: a laboratory machine often used to amplify segments of DNA using polymerase chain reaction.

tissue: a group or mass of similar cells working together to perform common functions.

toxin: a poisonous or harmful substance.

trait: a characteristic.

transcription: the process in which DNA is used to make a strand of messenger RNA.

transfer RNA (tRNA): a type of RNA molecule that helps to decode messenger RNA's sequence into a protein.

translation: the process in which messenger RNA attaches to a ribosome and creates a protein.

ultraviolet light: a kind of light with short wavelengths. It can't be seen with the naked eye.

validate: to prove accurate.

variation: a different or distinct form or version of something.

virus: a non-living, microscopic particle that can cause disease.

white blood cells: blood cells that are part of the body's immune system. They protect against infection by destroying diseased cells and germs.

whole-genome shotgun sequencing: the processing of sequencing an organism's entire genome at one time.

X-ray: a powerful wave of energy that lets doctors see bones inside bodies.

METRIC CONVERSIONS

Use this chart to find the metric equivalents to the English measurements in this activity. If you need to know a half measurement, divide by two. If you need to know twice the measurement, multiply by two.

ENGLISH	METRIC	
1 inch	2.5	centimeters
1 foot	30.5	centimeters
1 yard	0.9	meter
1 mile	1.6	kilometers
1 pound	0.5	kilogram
1 teaspoon	5	milliliters
1 tablespoon	15	milliliters
1 cup	237	milliliters

RESOURCES

BOOKS

Arney, Kat. *Exploring the Human Genome*. Rosen YA, 2019.

Gerdes, Louise. *Human Genetics*. Greenhaven Press, 2014.

Harvey, Derek. *The Secret Life of Genes: Decoding the Blueprint of Life*. Firefly Books, 2019.

Levy, Janey. *The Human Genome Project*. Gareth Stevens Publishing, 2019.

Lew, Kristi. *Genetic Ancestry Testing*. Enslow Publishing, 2019.

Lew, Kristi. *Understanding the Human Genome*. Enslow Publishing, 2019.

Mooney, Carla. *Evolution: How Life Adapts to a Changing Environment*. Nomad Press, 2017.

Mooney, Carla. *Genetics: Breaking the Code of Your DNA*. Nomad Press, 2014.

Quackenbush, John. *The Human Genome: The Book of Essential Knowledge*. Charlesbridge, 2011.

WEBSITES

Genetics Home Reference
ghr.nlm.nih.gov

Human Genome Project Information Archive
web.ornl.gov/sci/techresources/
Human_Genome/index.shtml

Human Genome Resources at the NCBI
ncbi.nlm.nih.gov/genome/guide/human

Human Origins Project
nationalgeographic.com/explorers
/projects/human-origins

Human Origins, Smithsonian Institute
humanorigins.si.edu

Learn Genetics
learn.genetics.utah.edu

National Human Genome Research Institute
genome.gov

Understanding Evolution
evolution.berkeley.edu/evolibrary/home.php

The International Genome Sample Resource
internationalgenome.org

Your Genome
yourgenome.org

MUSEUMS AND PLACES TO VISIT

American Museum of Natural History: amnh.org

Carnegie Museum of Natural History: carnegiemnh.org

Harvard Museum of Natural History: hmnh.harvard.edu

SELECTED BIBLIOGRAPHY

Church, George. *Understanding the Genome.* Grand Central Publishing, 2002.

Harris, Eugene E. *Ancestors in Our Genome: The New Science of Human Evolution.* Oxford University Press, 2015.

Harvey, Derek. *The Secret Life of Genes: Decoding the Blueprint of Life.* Firefly Books, 2019.

Quakenbush, John. *The Human Genome.* Charlesbridge, 2011.

Richards, Julia E., and R. Scott Hawley. *The Human Genome, Third Edition.* Academic Press, 2010.

Ryan, Frank. *The Mysterious World of the Human Genome.* Prometheus Books, 2016.

Human Origins, Smithsonian Institute: humanorigins.si.edu

Learn Genetics: learn.genetics.utah.edu

National Human Genome Research Institute: genome.gov

Understanding Evolution: evolution.berkeley.edu/evolibrary/home.php

Your Genome: yourgenome.org

QR CODE GLOSSARY

page 6: youtube.com/watch?v=AhsIF-cmoQQ

page 22: genome.gov/genetics-glossary/Genetic-Code

page 22: uniprot.org

page 37: youtube.com/watch?v=H0z8CSokkjU&feature=youtu.be

page 39: genomesize.com

page 45: encodeproject.org

page 72: youtube.com/watch?v=AXi68Qp3hQ0

page 74: ncbi.nlm.nih.gov/books/NBK100661

page 75: ncbi.nlm.nih.gov/books/NBK379478

page 75: ncbi.nlm.nih.gov/books/NBK84114

page 75: ncbi.nlm.nih.gov/books/NBK100660

page 75: ncbi.nlm.nih.gov/books/NBK84174

page 86: hhmi.org/biointeractive/biology-skin-color

page 87: genographic.nationalgeographic.com/human-journey

page 93: scientificamerican.com/video/what-is-a-genetically-modified-food2013-07-24

page 97: youtube.com/watch?v=McVwgeHa1Fk

page 98: vimeo.com/108260608

page 104: youtube.com/watch?time_continue=19&v=A5rUC6NiQfo

page 106: nc2.neb.com/NEBcutter2

INDEX

A

activities (Inquire & Investigate)
To Catch a Thief, 108–109
Create a Personalized
Medicine Brochure, 76–77
Cut With Molecular
Scissors, 106–107
Decoding DNA's Message, 22
Extract DNA from a
Strawberry, 7
Genome Testing for
the Athlete, 105
How Big Is Your Genome?, 39
How Mutations Occur, 56
Investigate Genetic
Variation, 54–55
Natural Selection, 90
Pharmacogenomics: How
the Genome Affects Drug
Response, 74–75
Spot a Cancer Mutation, 78
adenine, 12, 13, 19, 24
alleles, 11, 16, 17–18
amino acids, 19–20, 22
Ancestry.com, 96
assembler software, 28–29
autoimmune diseases,
16, 17, 64, 70, 99
automatic sequencing
machines, vi, 27, 29

B

bioinformatics, 52–53

C

Caenorhabditis elegans
genome, vii, 31
cancer, 17, 33, 51, 61, 64–68,
69–70, 72, 78, 98–99, 101
Cancer Genome Atlas, 65, 69
Celera Genomics, 36–37

cells
cell cycle/cell division, 13
definition of, 10
genes in, 4–5, 7, 10–17, 19–
21. *See also* DNA; genes
number and types
of, 10–11, 19
structure of, 11
Chargaff, Erwin, 19
chromosomes, 14–16,
30, 31, 33, 45, 49
circulating tumor DNA (ctDNA), 64
clone-by-clone sequencing, 25–26
CODIS (Combined DNA
Index System), 95
Collins, Francis, 36–37
comparative genomics, 49–52
Crick, Francis, vi, 19
crime scene analysis, vi, 94–95,
101, 102, 108–109
CRISPR, vii, 100–102
cystic fibrosis, vi, 36, 59, 67, 101
cytosine, 12, 13, 19, 24

D

denaturing and synthesizing, 32
Denisovans, vii, 81, 83
diabetes, 17, 62–64, 73, 100
direct-to-consumer genomic
testing, 95–97, 105
DNA (deoxyribonucleic acid)
ancient, vi–vii, 81, 82–86, 88
cells containing, 4–5,
7, 10–17, 19–21
circulating tumor, 64
decoding, vi, 19–22, 32–33
decomposing, 84–85
definition of, 7
denaturing and
synthesizing, 32
discovery of, vi, 15, 19
editing or changing, vii,
99–102, 106–107

external/environmental
influences on, 17–18,
47, 49, 51, 56, 62–63,
67, 97–99
forensic crime scene
analysis with, vi, 95,
101, 102, 108–109
genetic variations in, 47–49,
54–55, 68–69, 87–89
genome made of, 4–5, 39.
See also human genome
health and. *See* health
and disease
identical twins', 12, 21, 67
mutated, vii, 38, 51–52, 56,
58–62, 64–70, 72–74,
78, 87–89, 99–102
noncoding, 5, 30,
43, 44, 45–46
PCR technology
copying, vi, 31–32
replication of, 13
sequencing, vi, 25–30,
36–37, 78
structure of, vi, 12, 19, 24
dominant traits, 11, 18

E

ENCODE (Encyclopedia of
DNA Elements), vii, 45–46
epigenetics, 97–99. *See also*
external/environmental
influences
Ethical, Legal, and Social
Implications (ELSI)
Research Program, 103
ethical issues, 102–104
evolution. *See* human evolution
exons, 44
external/environmental
influences, 17–18, 47, 49,
51, 56, 62–63, 67, 97–99

INDEX

F

food and nutrition, 18, 88–89, 93–94
forensic crime scene analysis, vi, 94–95, 101, 102, 108–109
Franklin, Rosalind, vi, 19
Fraser, Claire, 29

G

gel electrophoresis, 26–28
genes. *See also* DNA;
   human genome
   C. elegans, 31
   cells containing, 4–5, 7, 10–17, 19–21
   chromosomes and, 14–16, 33, 45. *See also* chromosomes
   definition of, 4
   editing or changing, vii, 99–102, 106–107
   external/environmental influences on, 17–18, 47, 49, 51, 56, 62–63, 67, 97–99
   gene annotation, 43
   gene prediction, 43
   gene regulation, 16–17, 46, 63
   genetic adaptations, 81–82, 88–89
   genetic code, 19–22
   genetic diseases, vi, 58–61, 69, 98–99
   genetic traits, 11, 17–18, 81–82, 84, 86–90. *See also* physical traits
   genetic variations, 47–49, 54–55, 68–69, 87–89
   health and. *See* health and disease
   H. influenzae, 29–30
   inheritance of, vi, 4, 11, 14, 16, 81–82, 84
   mutated, vii, 38, 51–52, 56, 58–62, 64–70, 72–74, 78, 87–89, 99–102

number of, 4–5, 38, 43, 45
Genetic Information Nondiscrimination Act (2008), 103
genome browser, 46
genome-wide association study (GWAS), 72–73
genomic medicine, 68–70, 97. *See also* pharmacogenomics
genomics, 4. *See also* human genome
GMOs (genetically modified organisms), 93–94
guanine, 12, 13, 19, 24

H

Haemophilus influenzae genome, vi, 29–30
haplotypes, 49
health and disease. *See also specific diseases*
   bioinformatics data management on, 53
   comparative genomics and, 49, 51
   discrimination for potential issues of, 103
   external/environmental influences on, 18, 51, 56, 62–63, 67, 98–99
   food and nutrition, 18, 88–89, 93–94
   gene mutations and, vii, 38, 56, 58–62, 64–70, 72–74, 78, 87–89, 99–102
   genetic diseases, vi, 58–61, 69, 98–99
   genetic traits and, 17, 18, 87–89
   genetic variations and, 47, 49, 68–69, 87–89
   genome editing and, vii, 99–102
   genome-wide association study on, 72–73

genomic medicine for, 68–70, 97. *See also* pharmacogenomics
H. influenzae genome and, 29–30
human genome applications to, 33, 36–38, 43, 46, 57–78, 87–89, 92, 96–102
personalized medicine for, 68, 72, 76–77
pharmacogenomics and, 71–72, 74–75
polygenic disorders, 62–64
human evolution
   ancient DNA telling story of, vi–vii, 81, 82–86, 88
   definition of, 81
   fossils and archaeological evidence of, 81–87
   genetic adaptations and, 81–82, 88–89
   genetic mutation and diversity with, 87–89
   genetic traits and, 81–82, 84, 86–90
   human genome and, vi–vii, 79–90
   migration path and, vii, 85–87
   natural selection and, 88, 89, 90
human genome. *See also* DNA; genes
   bioinformatics data management on, 52–53
   comparison to other genomes, 49–52
   composition of, 3–4
   definition of, 2
   ENCODE catalog on, vii, 45–46
   ethical issues, 102–104
   exons and introns in, 44
   future applications of, 91–109
   genome browser/database, 46

INDEX

genome editing, vii,
99–102, 106–107
genome map of, vi–vii,
33–39. *See also* Human
Genome Project; 1000
Genomes Project
health improvements using.
See health and disease
history of mapping,
vi–vii, 5–6, 23–39
human evolution and,
vi–vii, 79–90
information in/from,
4–5, 41–56
noncoding regions of, 5,
30, 43, 44, 45–46
PCR technology and, 31–32
personal or direct-to-consumer
testing of, 95–97, 105
public vs. private access
to data on, 35–37, 45
reference genome, 26, 83
sequencing, 25–30,
36–38, 52, 65–68, 78
shared vs. distinct elements
of, 3, 46, 47–52, 86
size of, 39
smaller genomes sequenced
before, vi–vii, 29–31
structure of, 12, 29
Human Genome Project (HGP)
bioinformatics data
management in, 53
Celera project vs., 36–37
ELSI Research Program, 103
funding for, 36
future studies building on, 92
gene search in, 43–45
information from, 41–56
PCR technology in, 32
public access to, 35, 37
timeline of, vi–vii, 33–37

I

identical twins, 12, 21, 67
informed consent, 103
Innocence Project, 101
International HapMap
Project, vii, 47–49, 73
introns, 44

M

Mendel, Gregor, vi, 11
Miescher, Johann Friedrich, vi, 15
mitosis, 13
Mullis, Kary, vi, 31
mutated genes, vii, 38, 51–52,
56, 58–62, 64–70, 72–74,
78, 87–89, 99–102

N

nanopore DNA sequencing, 25
natural selection, 88, 89, 90
Neanderthals, 84–85, 88
nucleosomes, 14
nucleotides, 12, 13, 19–20,
24, 48–49, 51

O

1000 Genomes Project,
vii, 43, 44, 88

P

PCR (polymerase chain reaction)
technology, vi, 31–32
personal genomic testing,
95–97, 105
personalized medicine,
68, 72, 76–77
pharmacogenomics,
71–72, 74–75
physical traits, 2, 4, 15–16, 17–18,
52, 54–55, 81–82, 86, 102
polygenic disorders, 62–64

PopHumanScan project, 88
privacy issues, 103–104
progeria, 59–61
proteins, 4–5, 11, 12, 14–16,
19–20, 22, 30, 44, 45–46,
51, 61, 97–98, 100
Punnett square, 17

R

recessive traits, 11, 18
reference genome, 26, 83
RNA (ribonucleic acid), 20, 44

S

Sanger sequencing method,
vi, 26–27, 37
selective breeding, 93–94
selective sweep, 52
shotgun sequencing, 26, 36
single nucleotide polymorphism
(SNP), 48–49, 74

T

telomeres, 15
thymine, 12, 13, 19, 20, 24
transcription, 20, 22
23andMe.com, 96–97

U

UniProt database, 22
Universal Genetic Code, 22
uracil, 20

V

Venter, J. Craig, 29, 36

W

Wartman, Lukas, 66–68
Waterston, Robert, 33
Watson, James, vi, 19, 34
Wilkins, Maurice, 19